The English Home

By the same author:

LONDON: THE YEARS OF CHANGE
BRITAIN UNDER THE ROMANS
THE VOICE OF PROTEST

HAROLD PRIESTLEY

The English Home

FREDERICK MULLER

First published in Great Britain 1970
by Frederick Muller Ltd., Fleet Street, London, E.C.4

Copyright © 1970 Harold Priestley

Printed and bound in Great Britain by

Garden City Press Ltd., Letchworth, Hertfordshire

SBN: 584 10076 0

CONTENTS

ILLUSTRATIONS

LINE DRAWINGS

ACKNOWLEDGEMENTS

I should like to express my sincere thanks to Mr. Frank Sainsbury, Deputy Librarian of the London Borough of Newham, for his help and interest, to Mr. Fred Lees for reading the proofs, and to my wife for her assistance in the typing and preparation of the manuscript.

FOREWORD

It is hard to think of the term "The Homes of England" without the word "stately" springing to mind. The stately homes, however, do not nor ever have constituted more than a minute fraction of one per cent of the whole, and have already been well recorded both pictorially and descriptively. As one of the earliest researchers into the history of the English home says:

> "English writers on domestic architecture have been content for the most part with describing the remains of great villas, or the picturesque timber houses which adorn some of our old cities. Such buildings are more attractive to the casual eye than wattled huts or combinations of dwelling-house and cattle-stall. And yet, if we would learn how the masses of the English people lived in past times, we must not omit these plainer, but assuredly not less interesting buildings."[1]

The great drawback is that so many of the humbler dwellings have disappeared. Castles and manor-houses were built to last. In most cases their destruction could only be brought about by a deliberate act. Even some of the materials of which they were constructed are still to be found in more modern buildings. The hovel, the hut and the smaller house were much less durable. A violent storm, a flood, a careless accident with fire, and they might disappear, leaving no trace behind. For this reason the smaller house more than three hundred years old is rare, and one has to fall back on pictures, descriptions and the findings of archaeologists.

During the present century various causes have combined to set a definite limit to the frontiers of the home, a limit

---

[1] *The Evolution of the English House,* by S. O. Addy (Swan Sonnenschein, 1910)

which is best illustrated by the wide difference that exists between life in the old-fashioned village and life in the suburb. In the former, as parish records bear witness to all who have had no personal experience of it, one had to rely a great deal on the goodwill and help of neighbours in all the major crises of life. When Jack had a stroke or Jill came into money, the whole community reacted. Today, when Jack returns from work on a Friday evening, he can shut himself off from the world behind his garden fence or with his TV set. Today Jill may die alone in her apartment or small bungalow without her neighbours knowing anything about it until three or four milk bottles remain untouched on her front doorstep and the police are called to break in.

This implies no commendation of the past or condemnation of the present, for there are many other factors on both sides to be taken into account. In the Middle Ages, charity was accompanied by a deep callousness to human suffering, while today public concern about neighbourhood planning represents a promising effort to draw communities together. These facts are merely put forward to show that home is not bounded by the garden fence. Any book dealing with it must therefore treat of the house in its relation not only with the immediate environment but also with the social and political history of the country. This is what I have tried to do.

H.E.P.

The English Home

I

A Roof and Four Walls

The home of the primitive food-gathering man was the territory over which he ranged in search of a living; his refuge from the wild creatures which infested it was probably in the trees or in shelters of thickly interlaced boughs. His first permanent dwelling-place was the cave, its entrance perpetually guarded by fire, the "terrible red flower" from which all other jungle creatures fled, but which he alone had learnt to coax into being and to control. The red flames stood him in good stead during the cold phases of the Ice Age, when the vast ice-sheets and glaciers cut and moulded the surface of Britain, while animal life first fled southwards, then advanced again as the ice retreated, the days of the hair-clad mammoth alternating with those of the hippopotamus. Out of the long-drawn-out ebb and flow of the ice, Britain emerged, a temperate country, separated from the rest of Europe by the North Sea which swept across the sinking fens, and by the great Channel fault. Thus it became an island, inhabited by hunters using weapons tipped with flint, and following their quarry with dogs.

Meanwhile great changes were taking place elsewhere. In the Middle East, men had begun to keep sheep and cattle for draught and milk. They tilled the land and gathered harvests, gradually discovering and mastering more involved techniques such as spinning and weaving, the making of pots, the use of the plough and the wheel, and finally the intricate processes of smelting, hammering and casting metals. By 3,000 B.C. man had already emerged as a trader and a city-dweller in the valleys of the Nile and the Tigris-Euphrates, building houses of rammed earth and sun-baked brick as well as shrines and terraced temples.

In this technological revolution Western Europe lagged far behind, for it took many generations before a knowledge of metals and the skill to fashion tools from them penetrated to the far north-west. Even when it was acquired, it made little difference to the form of the early dwellings of Britain, firstly because both Briton and Saxon were by nature countrymen with no conception of town life, and secondly because they had in timber a material suited in every way to their limited needs. The Saxon word *getimbriam*, to build, is cognate with the German *Zimmer*, a room, as well as the Latin *domus*, a house. Stone, as an important building material, was hardly used at all in Britain before the coming of the Romans or within a couple of centuries of their departure.

Early man, like his primitive counterpart today, must have made use of whatever growing shoots or trees were at hand to build his dwellings and, as with the forest shelter, closely woven on a framework of straight boughs all propped against a central roof-tree, these early dwellings were probably for the most part circular. For the natural tree, Neolithic man in England substituted a central vertical pole to support the roof of his pit-dwelling. This was a flat-bottomed circular hole dug to a depth of about three feet in well-drained ground floored with clay and paved level with stones. Round the hole was raised a low wall of stones filled in with earth, and on this rested the lower ends of the long straight boughs which sloped upwards to the top of the centre-pole. A thatch of turves completed the structure, which was entered by a small opening sunk in one of its sides.

The round huts of small communities in the Middle and New Stone Ages must have been dotted all over the more open parts of England. Here, on the heathlands overlooking the denser forest and marsh of the valleys, the Neolithic farmer kept his lean cattle and sheep and reaped his meagre wheat harvests while his womenfolk carried on their simple domestic industries, softening, cutting and sewing skins, building up bowls and jars from long coils of clay without the aid of the potter's wheel and grinding their grain simply by crushing and rubbing it with a small hand-stone on a larger block slightly hollowed out by constant wear. These people were by no means isolated from other human contacts, for most of them lay within reach of the well-worn tracks which crossed the chalk, flint and other lighter soils, the principal ones radiating from the true centre of neolithic England – Salisbury Plain.

One of the earliest settled homes,
the neolithic hut

Whether sunk into the ground or put up on its surface, the circular hut was easier to erect than any other, needing only a number of poles of equal length and an amount of rough thatching material. In more recent times charcoal burners have made their temporary shelters on the same principle, drawing together thin poles into the shape of a cone, interlacing them with wattle, then, leaving a small hole for a doorway, covering the construction with sods. The same kind of primitive hut has been found with minor variations all over Europe.

Even in regions where timber was scarce, the circular building tended to predominate. Flat stones or blocks of baked earth could be piled in ever-narrowing circles, keyed, or capped at the apex, the crevices stopped up with earth and the whole construction plastered over with mud which in turn became overgrown in the same way as on the Teutonic pit-hut. This bee-hive construction was to be found in the more northerly and treeless regions of the British Isles as well as in parts of the Middle East. While the round hut or beehive cell was the simplest to erect, the only way to enlarge it was to build a second cell adjacent to it, opening into it by a doorway

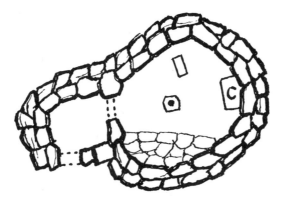

Plan of neolithic pit dwelling with side entrance and stone bench

common to both. Double beehive cells, connected in this manner, are to be found in Scotland and Ireland, while in southern Italy today the multiple round-house appears in its most complicated form. The landscape of Apulia is dotted with these strange structures known as *trulli*. Each unit is a beehive hut built of dry stone and whitewashed, one small room, connected with four or five others like it to form a complete house.

A multiple round house of southern Italy in use in the middle ages and still inhabited

The most detailed picture we possess of life in a community of circular houses is that of the so-called lake village of Glastonbury. Strictly speaking it was not a lake village, for whereas the true lake villages of an earlier period in Switzerland and other parts of Europe were built on piles driven into the lake beds, Glastonbury and many others in the British Isles were constructed on marshy ground probably subject to flooding in the wet seasons of the year. On a foundation of logs and lopped trunks laid in the marsh, one layer at right angles across another, in some places to a thickness of 4 ft., an artificial island was built up with clay, gravel, heather, brushwood and ferns. The island was defended by a strong palisade of thick poles driven close together into the soft bottom of the rushy mere and interwoven by hurdles. The whole island was floored with large pieces of timber placed side by side to a depth of about a foot, and on this substructure the houses were raised. Their walls were on a framework of upright posts about one foot apart, interwoven with withies and made into a construction of wattle and daub, supporting a roof of thatch. A few slabs of stone were laid down at the entrances and each house had its hearth of stone or clay in the centre of the floor. The alley-ways between the huts were paved with cobbles, and there were thresholds of irregularly-placed blocks of stone.

Here, concealed by thick natural screens of elders and willows and protected by surrounding stretches of fen, the village might lie hidden while an invading enemy ranged over the nearby countryside. Even if discovered, it would not be easily taken by men unused to life among the marshes. At times when it was undisturbed, members of the little community could make a good livelihood, cultivating corn and vegetable crops on the open land within reach, and with an ample supply of fish and game.

"Inside its protecting wall, the village itself is full of life and activity—a compact stronghold of humanity isolated among the swamps. Duck and coot can be heard calling and splashing among the reeds where herons and cranes stand

motionless; occasionally a bittern sounds its uncanny, boom-
ing call; and there, top-heavy, comical and grotesquely
beautiful, a family of pelicans is sailing down the open water-
way. The villagers naturally avail themselves of all this wild
life over their fence to add seasonable variety to their meals:
they enjoy wildfowl of many kinds, especially duck, and
also such freshwater fish as perch, roach and trout."[1]

While the Glastonbury lake village was still in existence
other dwellings, both circular and rectangular in shape, were
occupied by some British farmers and continued to exist all
through the Roman era, while other farmers abandoned their
old ways and, taking down their primitive huts, replaced them
with the more advanced rectangular constructions which later
developed into small villas in the Roman style. Excavations on
the sites of Roman villas have revealed traces of the circular
huts that preceded them. Groups of such British huts have
been discovered by air reconnaissance on the chalk downland
not far from Salisbury and in many other places. Some take
the form of enclosures in which stand the large hut of the
owner and the smaller ones used as dwellings, sheds and workshops by his dependants. Around such a settlement lay the
irregularly shaped Celtic fields in which the crops grew. Such
was the homestead of the small British farming community.
Poorer Britons who were largely uninfluenced by contact with
their rulers also lived in such small circular huts. The remains
of a group of four, measuring between eleven and twenty feet
in diameter, were found preserved under the Thames mud on
the foreshore at East Tilbury in Essex.

The Saxons, too, had huts that were circular in shape.
Tacitus, describing the dwellings of these tribes before they
crossed from northern Germany, says they were accustomed
to make artificial caves in the ground which they covered with
great heaps of dung. These they used as storehouses during the
summer and as shelter during the winter months. They were

---

[1] *Prehistoric Britain,* Christopher and Jacquetta Hawkes (Chatto & Windus, 1937).

inconspicuous and less liable to attack, for, says Tacitus, the enemy "ravages the parts that he can see, but either discovers not such places as are invisible and subterraneous, or else the delay such search would cause is a protection to the inmates". These were without doubt circular and the same kind of building was employed when the tribes reached England. At Pakenham in Norfolk the remains of some of these huts have been found, sunk from eighteen inches to two feet into gravelly well-drained ground, and from seven feet upwards in diameter. Their roofs were probably of boughs drawn together round a ridge pole and they were thatched with reeds and turves. In them were found the remains of domestic pursuits— hearths of stone and red pebbles which had probably been heated in the fire and dropped into water to bring it to the boil. Stone benches round the sides and raised couches of gravel showed that these had been used for sleeping. Other Saxon hut-dwellings have yielded the remains of the work of smith, weaver and potter.

Here is seen another aspect of the home, that of a place to work in. Hardly existing at first, it grew to greater and greater significance as the ages passed by. In all civilisations the farmer and craftsman have produced their wares at home. Women spun yarn sitting in the sun by their doors; the medieval farmer stored his corn and made his butter and cheese either in his homestead or the adjacent buildings, and the craftsman's apprentices worked in his shop while his wife busied herself in the house behind it. A house was then not only a dwelling, but also a workshop.

In the days of the Romans, Britain was made up socially of two worlds, and these were reflected in the types of buildings that existed. The first type was the native homestead composed of circular and rectangular huts enclosed in a compound. Its owner might have been untouched by contacts with Rome except when the taxgatherer or the provincial governor made demands on him. Away from the direct routes of the Roman roads there were many such. Even in the more populous south and east of the country some native farmers, either through poverty or the force of tradition, never adopted the Roman four-walled type of building.

The second world was that of the town, the military base and the seaport, including places along the lines where traffic and trade took place. Here lived the shopkeepers, the artisans, the officials, the innkeepers and traders and the gentlemen. Though many of these were of British stock, they spoke Latin and were romanised. Excavations have revealed towns with streets lined with workplaces and shops, houses with porches, colonnades and verandas, centrally heated by hypocausts circulating hot air under floors and in walls, and, on a larger scale, imposing temples, market-places and basilicas. Dotted about the countryside, especially in central southern Britain, were the villas, large and small, some consisting of a line of rooms with a southerly aspect, others making a complete square round a quadrangle. Grouped about the main building were numerous outhouses for horses, carriages and cattle, while further away, scattered over the estates of these villas would be the hovels inhabited by the slaves who laboured on them.

When the Romans occupied Britain they superimposed one technique on another more primitive one. They were skilled in building and engineering and could create halls, roads, public works and other elements necessary to the administration of an imperial province on a scale impossible to the native Briton. For their purposes they used any materials at hand. They combined timber, burnt brick and stone. Where stone was lacking they took the pebbles and flinty earth and, with cement made from limestone, septaria or seashells, constructed walls of conglomerate strengthened with strings of rose-coloured tiles. The remains of the ingenuity and industry may still be seen in the walls of Colchester, the rugged pavements, good after two thousand years, which cross the Pennines, villas such as those at Chedworth, Woodchester and Lullingstone, the remains of the Great Wall, the Newport Gate of Lincoln and other relics.

The Saxon, whose natural background was the small agricultural community, had no use for the buildings the Romans left behind. Neither the town house nor the country villa with their quadrangles and verandas, their bare walls and high, airy rooms had any attraction for him as places to live in. He far preferred the cosy intimacy of the smoke-filled hut. Thus Britain went back, or nearly back to the beginning. The villas which had not gone up in flames were allowed to fall into decay, towns ceased any longer to be towns, though as local markets they continued to function because of their accessibility by way of the now neglected Roman roads, most of which still survived and many of which became avenues of Saxon settlement. On the Saxon level, trade was as easy to carry on in a disused overgrown street as in the best-organized forum. The supplanting of the Roman way of life by that of the less advanced Saxon meant that in the history of the English home four centuries of technological progress were completely wiped out, and it was almost as if they had never existed.

For the houses of the Saxons we therefore go back to first principles in the building of shelters, both circular and rectangular. The low vertical sides of some of these huts were underground and the superstructure was raised on a frame of two pairs of poles rising from each corner to meet on a central line, their apices fastened to a long ridge pole which ran along that line. This construction, which had also been used by the Britons, had one great advantage in that it could be extended by doubling or multiplying its length, whereas the circular hut could neither be extended easily on ground level nor by adding an upper storey. For this reason as a permanent dwelling the circular hut had no future.

The peoples of the Germanic mainland of Europe are known to have built rectangular houses on this plan 15-18 ft. wide and sometimes as many as 90 ft. long. The "long house" of 90 ft. would generally be raised on about seven pairs of supports, each enclosing a "bay" of 15 ft.

The Saxons were seafaring people who, when they settled in England, applied their knowledge of shipbuilding and carpentry to the creation of farmsteads. From the earliest times the need of the nomadic groups to defend themselves from marauders had given them what the Britons had in large measure lacked–a strong sense of community and the ability to work together. Their ships were built by joint effort and their village agriculture was organized in the same way, on a co-operative basis. With the axe as their principal tool they made clearings in the forests and hewed the large tree trunks to build their great halls. These were buildings which furnished shelter for horses and cattle as well as people, while their barns housed their crops and farm implements. Whereas the Britons, who had farmed on a much more individual if not always on a smaller scale, had been content with simpler constructions based on stays lashed together with thongs, the Saxons knew how to square their timbers and lock them together with mortise and tenon joints and to fasten them with pegs.

In this way a firm, box-like frame could be put together, made up of as many bays as were needed, and the great rafters could be made to lean on it so that they met along a ridge. The rafters were supported near the base by shorter posts which carried purlins and themselves rested on wooden sills laid on the ground or raised on low walls of stone or rubble. Near the ridge the rafters were strengthened by a ridge beam carried on kingposts, the ridge beam itself supporting as many collar-beams as there were pairs of rafters, each collar-beam stretching from one rafter to its fellow opposite. It is believed that in these constructions the two end bays were not spanned by rafters but were filled in at the sides with wattle and daub and secured at the end by large doors of wooden planks which, open during the daytime, let in the light. The whole construction was thatched with turf, heather, reeds or whatever material was to hand, leaving only two triangular holes where the rafters ended, and through these some of the smoke escaped from the fire which burned in the centre of the hall.

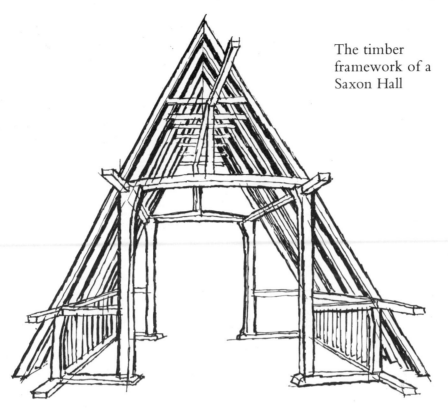

The timber
framework of a
Saxon Hall

Round such a hall as this the whole life of the early Saxon
community revolved. It was an all-purpose building well
suited to the needs of its owner. The far end was reserved for
him and his family who ate at the high table and slept in the
adjacent space. The rest of the household, relatives, guests and
principal officers dined from trestles which were cleared away
when the meal was over. Food was cooked in the open air and
carried into the hall to be eaten. At nightfall the hall presented
a different spectacle. The oxen and horses were brought in and
stabled in the bays between the short posts supporting the
lower ends of the long rafters, while above them slept the
servants of the household, men on one side of the hall and
women on the other. The distance between these posts, that is,
the breadth of a bay, was the space required for four oxen
either standing in the stall or harnessed four abreast to the

plough. It was such a common unit of measurement that it is said to have been the original length of the rod – $5\frac{1}{2}$ yards. The acre covers a space equal to a strip of land 4 rods or one chain (22 yards) broad and 220 yards (one furrow-long or furlong) in length. Thus the dimensions not only of the parts of the Saxon hall, but also the units of land measurement before the coming of the decimal system may have been fixed by the amount of room required for standing or driving four oxen.

Near to the hall with its palisaded courtyard and outbuildings would be the village, made up of the hovels of the common people. Every one was a farmer, cultivating the parts of the large common field assigned to him, and entitled to his share in the use of ploughs and teams, meadow pasture, the rough grazing on the waste and the wood, gravel, turves, reeds or other things of value that could be taken from it. In times of peace this was a small self-sufficing, hard-working community running its affairs according to ancient custom, in which every member worked and played an effective part.

This shape of building, with rafters sloping directly from the ground and resting on a box-like framework, must have been common in houses much smaller in size than the Saxon Hall. In the smallest, even the box framework might have been dispensed with, the house consisting only of rafters and ridgetree held together by tiebeams and purlins. A framework of this kind was easy to erect and even to carry from place to place, and wherever it was put up it could be thatched with local materials. S. O. Addy[1] says that buildings of this sort were used as summer dwellings by herdsmen when cattle in hilly districts were taken up to their summer pastures, and he derives such names as Somerscales and Summerlodge, both in Yorkshire, and many others with "summer" as a prefix, from this practice.

[1] *The Evolution of the English House.*

II

Ends and Means

Though we have nothing to tell us what the cote of the medieval English peasant was really like, we have every reason to believe that it was rectangular, usually of one bay only and that it varied little from early Saxon times to the end of the Middle Ages. The generally accepted picture of a medieval village shows the hovels thatched with turf, straw and reeds, each one enclosed within its toft or small plot of land, along the village street, together with the church, the manor hall inhabited by the lord or his bailiff set on its own small estate or demesne, and the manorial mill on the stream near the water meadows, while around the little settlement were the common fields, the rough pasture or waste and the encircling forest.

If we have in mind twentieth-century standards, the small, dark and smoky hovel of the medieval peasant must appear primitive and unpleasant, but it was nevertheless a home. The snug protection it gave from the extremes of climate was the measure of its comfort, and the straw pallet gave its occupant as much ease as the deepest armchair or divan of today. With its little yard it made a workplace where the men fashioned not only the farming tools they used, but also the simple articles of domestic use such as wooden benches, stools, dishes and platters, while the women peeled reeds for winter rush-lights, wove them into baskets, combed, carded and spun wool from the scraggy sheep they kept, made and mended garments with thread of hemp and nettle. A few fowls scratching in the toft provided them with eggs while on the common land their sheep and the lean cattle they kept, gave them meagre supplies of wool, meat and milk. In such a home lived fair Griseld of Chaucer's Clerk's Tale, a young maiden who "would not be idle till she slept" and by her hard work kept her poor father from starvation.

Langland's *Piers Plowman* throws light on the miserable lot of such people in bad days and hard winters, how they slaved to pay the rent demanded by their rapacious landlords, starving themselves to provide meal and milk for their crying children, lying awake at night racked with the pangs of hunger, and yet ashamed to beg.

The one drawback of a house built on a frame of sloping posts tied to a ridge pole was that it provided very little head-room for the persons inside. This led the builder to search for boughs that were slightly curved so that they could be set together to form, not a triangle, but an arch. If such boughs could be found thick and strong enough he would often take on the difficult task of sawing them in two down the middle so that when put up to meet one another at the apex they would form a perfect match. At first the posts were thrust straight into the ground, probably after having been charred at the lower ends to prevent rot, but it was afterwards found better to let them rest on specially prepared stone sills. In districts where stone was scarce, the sills were made of stout oak trunks laid on the ground along a line where the bottom ends of the posts were laid to rest. These naturally-curved beams are called crucks, and there are many cottages today in whose end walls the crucks may still be seen. Sometimes when a cottage is being pulled down its ancient cruck framework is laid bare beneath a covering of more recent brickwork.

To strengthen the cruck framework of a cottage, the sloping beams were linked together across the end by tie-beams and half way up along the length of the building by purlins. The spaces between these were probably filled in with suitably shaped branches overlaid with thatch of straw, brushwood, reeds or heather which covered the whole structure from the ridge-pole to the ground. The breadth of the building depended on the size of the crucks on which it was framed and its length on the number of bays which the crucks enclosed. The

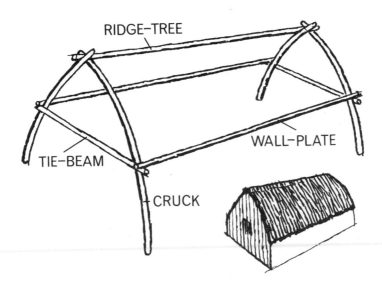

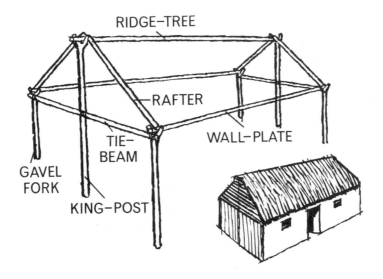

Construction of the medieval house

bay being normally a space of 16 ft., a building could be extended to any convenient multiple of this number, and could be further enlarged by making an offshoot at one or both ends. We can imagine the appearance of the interior of a building like this–the great curved beams visible on the inside to a height of about 14 ft. arching up towards the central ridge-pole, the whole roof-wall exposed to view with no ceiling, the light for the interior coming in only through the small doorway, the narrow "wind-eyes", or windows, and an additional opening in the roof through which some of the smoke from the hearth made its way out. The steep pitch of the roof made for a great deal of waste space overhead, the sloping sides lessened the headroom and the footage of useful space on ground level. What was needed was to lift the thatch well away from the ground by the addition of a vertical wall. This would lessen the pitch of the roof and leave more room for a second floor if necessary.

The problem was solved by extending the tie-beams so that their ends fell immediately over the bases of the crucks, supporting the ends by posts and connecting them together by lengths of wood known as wall plates which ran the length of

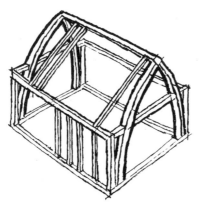

Cruck frame with extended tie beams and low vertical walls

the bay. This made it possible to run the rafters from the ridge-pole down to the wall plate, and to build the vertical wall up from the ground to reach it. Thus the wall created space but carried no weight since the whole weight of the roof was still borne by the crucks. In this way headroom was secured and it was made possible to put in an upper storey or loft, laying the floor of this on the level of the wallplate and leaving in it a hole so that it could be reached by a ladder from below. Here we have the origin of the small two-storey house.

The actual construction, the preparation and sawing of the beams was difficult enough in days when tools were not in an advanced state, but once this had been done, and the various parts joined together by pegs, it was not difficult to hoist the crucks into place, to fix on the wallplates and to complete the process of construction with wattle and daub for the walls and thatch for the roof. Prefabrication is by no means an innovation in building. Thus in many an instance moving house must have meant exactly what the words imply, taking down the house in parts and transporting it to another site, a task which involved considerably less trouble and expense than selling it and building another elsewhere.

Cruck construction was not the only way in which medieval man succeeded in putting a roof over his head. A section of the Bayeux Tapestry shows William the Conqueror and his army galloping from Pevensey towards Hastings. On the way they pass the homes of the local farmers and compel them to come out and slaughter their cattle for a Norman feast. There are in all pictures of three houses which have walls rising to more than half their height. Two of these appear to be overlaid with horizontal boards, while the roofs seem either to be thatched or covered with wooden shingles. The door of each house is arched and is placed in the middle of the house's length. The roofs of these three box-framed houses appear to be sloping, or hipped, with no gables.

One of the methods used by the Germanic peoples of supporting a roof was to erect a double row of posts running the length of the building, to tie them together with tie-beams and wall-plates and on this secure construction to raise the roof, which could be either gabled or hipped. This is the origin of what is known as the box-frame construction. The box-frame type of house has the advantage over the cruck in that, firstly, it would support a higher roof leaving more room for an upper storey, and secondly because of the higher walls and vertical supports it was possible to build offshoots not only at the ends of the main construction but along its length as well.

A primitive version of the hipped roof is found in the modern hut erected by the bark peelers in the Lake District who, having first erected a double wall about 2 ft. high of wattles, with the space between them packed tightly with earth, brought up from each corner four poles, tying their ends to a shorter ridge pole. This simple framework of a hipped roof was filled in by more slender poles resting on the ridge and supporting a thatch of overlapping turves, the grassy sides turned inwards. There was a hearth in the middle of one long side, a door in the other, and the two beds were placed in the enclaves at each end.

"In the old time," wrote William Harrison in 1587, "the houses of the Britons were slightly set up with few posts and many raddles, with stables and all offices under one roof, the like whereof almost is to be seen in the fenny countries and northern parts unto this day."

The old Germanic tradition of bringing men and animals under one roof continued all through the Middle Ages, for in most places only the lord could afford to build separate houses for his cattle and farm produce. In the north, farm servants or "hinds" occupied such houses. Addy (*The Evolution of the English House*) describes these "coits" or combined purpose dwellings, which were divided into bays either by crucks or by the pillars on which the roof was supported. The main part of the building, separated from the rest by an interior wall, consisted of a main floor for threshing and storage, with one part of it divided off into standing for cows. The end bay of the buildings consisted of one large room with fireplace against the outer wall, and behind it a store, in one corner of which a ladder gave access to a bedroom above. The living-room was connected by an inner door to the large floor from which the labourer could give the cows their winter feed without having to go outside.

Another common type was the "long house", a cruck-framed or box-framed construction made by increasing the number of bays. Here people, cattle, pigs and poultry all lived under one roof, so that it became a sort of inverted Noah's Ark. In the medieval long house, one end was set apart for human habitation and separated from the rest of the building by a dividing wall, while the part in which the stock lived was no more than a long dark shed whose earthen floor was fouled and made into a quagmire by the accumulation of animal excrement. Yet this sort of building served its purpose well, for it was highly convenient for the small farmer to have everything gathered together in one place. In Devonshire and Wales medieval long houses remained in occupation until the eighteenth century, when many new ones were built, some of which have lasted until the present day.

One of the oldest of all building materials is earth. Cut into turves for thatch, or mixed with water and daubed on to wattles, it served to protect early homes from the weather as far back as prehistoric times. Sheltered from downpours by a deep and ample thatch, it could be made to last a long time. From the days of the ancient Egyptians and Babylonians, earth was mixed with binding materials such as dung, hair, grasses and straw and used, either baked or unbaked, for walls. If unbaked, enough time was needed to enable it to set.

The Romans were expert tile-burners and the well-known rosy pink tiles they made, measuring roughly 18 in. by 9 in. by $1\frac{1}{2}$ in., formed the foundations and sills of houses and villas even in districts where stone was readily obtainable. To the people of Saxon and Norman times, especially in places where stone was scarce, the tiles from Roman buildings, especially if they could be found unbroken, were almost beyond price when it came to building up the angles of their rubble-filled walls. The mere fact that in a certain village or town a medieval church may be partly built with Roman tiles is no proof that the Romans once lived there, for in some parts of England, especially in the south-east, people must have travelled long distances to bring home cartloads of Roman tiles and fragments. In places of substantial Roman settlement they have been used both for strength and ornament in medieval buildings. Colchester alone has two very remarkable ones. The first is the Saxon church of the Holy Trinity, the angles of whose tower and the pointed triangular arch of whose door are made entirely of them. The second, St. Botolph's Priory, is a veritable marvel of medieval construction. Semi-circular Norman arches, not of stone but of rubble and flint tinged by numerous delicate pink fragments, rise one above the other, while the west front of the priory is intricately decorated with interlocking arches composed of thousands of Roman tiles, with a doorway within a fine semi-circular retiring arch of small thin bricks and hewn stone in alternate succession. Here the medieval masons made fine use of what the Romans had left. But although both Saxons and Normans used these remains, there is little evidence that, before the thirteenth century at least, they burnt many bricks or tiles for themselves.

As a building material, unbaked earth must have been used extensively, especially where wood was not plentiful. If it contains lime and a certain amount of binding materials it will serve for solid walls providing it rests on a sufficiently high plinth to act as a damp course. Cottages in Devon and Cornwall, smooth-cornered and with extremely thick walls, were built of this material, the Cornish cob strengthened with small pieces of slate known as shilf. Where today, largish houses of cob or other unbaked earth may still be seen (such as Raleigh's house at Hayes Barton in Devonshire), it is reasonable to believe that in olden times this was the material most in use for small cottages and hovels.

The building of a cob cottage was a laborious process, for the composition had to be carefully and throughly blended, laid to a depth of only a few inches unsupported by wooden shuttering, then well trodden down as it was placed in position. Before another layer was added, the former one had

Devonshire cob: a thatched cottage at Higher Aston, Devonshire

to be allowed to dry out completely, a process which took a fortnight even in favourable weather. What resulted was a solid construction, capable, if well thatched and protected from ground damp, of lasting, even for centuries. All over England, especially in the north-west and south-west, this kind of building must have been common in the Middle Ages, every house a small co-operative enterprise, one man helping his neighbour.

There are many variations in the composition of unbaked earth. In one part of Buckinghamshire the chalky earth which lies a little below the surface was used, mixed with straw to form a composition called wichert or witchet. In Roman times the Gauls of the Rhône valley built wooden shutters into which they rammed specially prepared earth mixed with a good measure of gravel and sand, and a small amount of sticky clay. Trodden well down, almost dry, the particles of the mixture adhered firmly to each other to make a solid wall. This kind of earth, still known by its French name of *pisé de terre* or pisé, is still used. In the days immediately following the last war, the dearth of building materials caused people again to experiment in the making of pisé and other forms of stabilised earths. Most English soil is suitable for mixtures of this kind though they are rarely found. What is more common especially in East Anglia is the clay lump, a blending of clay and straw well trodden and cut into blocks roughly 18 in. by 9 in. by 6 in., used for building in the same way as bricks and bound with fine wettish clay mortar. The history of all the methods of building with un-baked earths is unknown but some of them, especially mud and cob, must have been in use from very early times.

A long period of settlement was needed before the Saxons learnt how to quarry stone and shape it to their own purposes. Even their early religious buildings were probably of wood. The small church at Greensted in Essex is famous as the only survival of a log church in England. It is believed to have been built in the year 1013, when the monks of Bury halted there while carrying the remains of Saint Edmund from London to their final resting-place. The oak logs were split vertically into halves and set, the rounded sides inward, on an

An early form of wall construction in England was of logs set vertically on a ground sill. Greensted Church near Ongar, Essex

oak sill. This has since rotted away and has been replaced by brick, but the upper parts of the old logs still stand, the mark of the workman's adze still to be seen plainly on them. There are also references in documents to wooden churches at Wilton, Lewes and Chester-le-street, and although we have no definite proof it is quite possible that some Saxon halls were built in this way.

At first, stone was only used for "basing" or for the foundations of houses, and on it rested a wooden super-structure as had been the case in the Roman villa. There was, however, a quantity of trimmed and squared stone which had been left behind by the Romans, and before the Saxons tried their own hands at the stonemason's craft they certainly used much of this. But from small beginnings they eventually came to be skilful masons themselves and with that religious fervour that characterised early England in its greatest age they put the best of their work into the churches and monaster-ies. Some of these churches, or at least their towers, still stand.

The application of stone to the building of a hall probably came later, and here the old Saxon tradition of having a room underground or partially underground for a storage place or a workshop still persisted. Stone resists decay and was from the earliest times used for building up the walls of underground chambers. Even when the basement was not quite below ground level the Saxons used it for storage and made the first floor, reached by a flight of steps outside, the habitable part of their dwelling.

An early scene in the Bayeux tapestry shows Harold, after having prayed with his friend before the church at his manor of Bosham, sitting at table in the upper room of the manor house, over the arched chamber on the ground floor, while one of his captains beckons him to join the fleet at anchor near by and a second captain is going down the steps outside the hall. Halls of this kind, many of them built after the Norman conquest, are to be seen in many parts of England today, but most of them were not entirely of stone. At the time of the

Conqueror there were no stone houses in England, this material being reserved for sacred buildings, such as churches and monasteries, and some castles and palaces. As the centuries passed by it came into domestic use, especially in towns such as Stamford where it was plentiful. Of the surviving stone houses in England, only six or seven date from the twelfth century and 25 from the thirteenth.

III

The Medieval Home

The Norman conquest of England resulted in a general redistribution of property as English lords were dispossessed of their lands and Normans took their places. With the great transfer, a sudden impetus was given to building. First, the new lords required well-fortified strongholds, private fortresses in which they could keep men-at-arms to subdue their restless vassals or carry out raiding expeditions. *Hic fecit Robertus suum castellum*—"Here Robert built his castle"—is the sort of expression found in Domesday Book. The Latin word, diminutive of *castrum*, a camp, aptly describes this kind of construction. Most of them were nothing like the elaborate stone structures called to mind by the word "castle". The Norman lord chose the most suitable place—a rounded hillock, a bluff, or perhaps the ready-made site of an old British or Saxon fort, protected by the remains of ditch and rampart. The making of a fortress on such a site was a simple enough matter given plenty of labour. The top of the mound was levelled to make a courtyard, and the ditch was deepened. The earth which had been dug out was used to increase the angle of slope of the outer fortification, and to throw up an inner one to which the captain and a picked number of his men could retire in case they had to make a last stand. This "fort inside a fort" was called the *motte* (French, a moated mound), and the larger enclosure below it the bailey (Latin *ballium*).

Both were defended by strong palisades. The outer fortification or bailey could be entered by going across a bridge over the ditch and ascending a narrow road which sloped up the rampart towards a gap in the stockade. All the buildings on this enclosed space would be of wood, possibly with foundations of stone or rubble. In addition to a small hall, there would be hutments for the garrison, stabling for the horses, kitchens near to the hall, latrines and refuse dumps along the side of the palisade. In many places the fort overlooked a small peaceful village or town whose houses and huts were grouped round the market place or along the main street.

Some forts, generally those built by the kings and principal lords, were much more elaborate. The Normans brought from the Continent improved methods of building in stone. To erect their strongholds many of them had to have it carried from distant places. One of the first things William the Conqueror did after taking London was to clear away part of the Roman wall on the eastern side of the city and make a fortified post. On this spot his son William Rufus began the construction of the White Tower, a large square fortress which served as a model for all the early stone forts in England at the time. It is built mainly of Kentish ragstone except for the dressings for which freestone was brought from Caen in Normandy. Other castles were sited at strategic points, notably Norwich and Colchester. In the eleventh century smaller rectangular keeps of this kind were built, surviving examples of which are Castle Hedingham in Essex, whose facings are of stone from Barnack in Northamptonshire, Burgh Castle in Suffolk with its walls of flint and mortar, and Rochester Castle, built of Magnesian limestone brought from the Pennines. In constructing these formidable towers, even more reliance was placed on their strength than on their situation, for their walls, ten feet and more in thickness, were so solid as to hold out against any but the most vigorous and long-drawn out assaults, even by battering rams, and it was hard to undermine them. These heavily fortified communities, for such they were, dominated everything around them and their occupants lived in another world from that of the poor peasants of the adjacent villages.

This kind of rectangular stone keep was in some ways like the hall in which Harold is seen feasting in the Bayeux Tapestry. The main similarity is in the living-room, which again is on the first floor and is reached by an outer stair. This made for greater security, for to enter the keep an enemy had to ascend that stair in face of fire from the upper window-openings, and had to break down the door in full view of the defenders. There was no entry to the ground floor which was used as storage space, except by way of a stair from the inside. The floor of the main living-room, at least in the larger keeps, was of flagged stone so that a fire could be lit on it, and it was supported by a vaulted undercroft in the basement. The great hall was itself spanned by a wide arch, and this held up the wooden floor of the upper story. Some of these Norman keeps had rounded angles which contained spiral stone stair-ways and small dark corners used as bedrooms.

At the time of the redistribution of England by William the Conqueror, the economic unit was the feudal estate or manor (manerium), held either directly or indirectly from the king by its lord. Some great barons and religious houses held large numbers of such manors dotted about the country and employed resident bailiffs to look after their affairs and stewards to pay regular visits, to examine accounts and to collect dues. Every manor of any size had its own hall in which lived the bailiff or, if the manor was not part of a large noble's domains, the lord himself. Thus, though England's castles were the strongest buildings in the country, they were not as important as the manor-houses, for in these smaller establishments, each the centre of a busy little community, the wealth of the country was produced and garnered.

The manor houses, of which there must have been large numbers in the hundred years following the Norman conquest, were modest enough places. Some, of one storey only, consisted usually of a "house-part" or entry hall, the only room with an outer door where, on ordinary days the household dined. On special occasions, however, they went with their guests through the door leading out of it into the large hall, the eating and sleeping place for the men on festive and formal occasions. On the other side of the house-part was the bower or "maydens" house, a common feature in all medieval houses of any size. Some smaller houses consisted only of hall and bower, the house-part being omitted altogether.

The rooms were large by modern standards. The hall at Kensworth, Herts, measured 35 ft. by 30 ft. and was 22 ft. high, 11 ft. from tie-beams to ridge-tree. The house-part, the smallest room of all, was 12 ft. by 17 ft. and the bower 22 ft. by 16 ft. Each small manor-house had its appropriate out-buildings such as stables, servants' quarters, bakehouses, storehouses for grain and usually the kitchen, often separate from the main building or arranged within a lean-to. The natural arrangement of these outhouses was a quadrangle, part of one side of which was taken up by the main building, whose front door and larger windows faced inwards. This form was largely dictated by the need for defence. In parts of the country open to attack, the thick defensive wall of a manor house might enclose space of some 5 to 6 acres, suf-ficient to drive in the owner's cattle in time of danger. As might be expected, the outer window openings of these mini-ature fortressess were small, for even where the countryside was beautiful the builders rated the view of fine scenery far below the requirements of personal safety.

Some manor-houses had two storeys. The one at Padley Hall near Hathersage in Derbyshire had a hall and buttery on the ground floor and a bower and chapel over it. Others, notably in south-west England, were of one story only. Of the Cornish manor-houses Richard Carew wrote in 1602, "The ancient manner of Cornish building was to plant their houses lowe, to lay the stones with mortar of lyme and sand, to make the walles thick, their windows arched and little, and their lights inwards to the court. . . . Thus the pleasure of seeing was sacrificed for the advantage of not being seen."

It is probable that long before this time some people had

Twelfth-century house at Boothby Pagnell,
Lincolnshire, with separate bedchamber at one end
(far right)

built the walls of their houses in stone, though in the eleventh
century it was not the primary building material for the smaller house. In the twelfth and succeeding centuries, however,
especially in the stone-bearing districts of England, stone
manor houses with external steps, vaulted undercrofts and
first-floor living accommodation, were built in greater
numbers. These, too, were centres of small rural communities
revolving round the lord of the manor and his family or, if
he were an absentee, round that of his steward or bailiff, and
they consisted of manorial servants, officials and labourers,
while outside the precincts would be the homes of the tenants
grouped along or around the main thoroughfare.

Stone houses also began to appear in the towns. The Jews'
houses of Lincoln and Bury St. Edmunds are examples of
early stone domestic town buildings. They followed the
fashion of the larger ones, the ground floor being for storage

and the first floor, probably open to the roof, the only living-room in the house, one end probably divided off by a screen or partition. The twelfth century also saw a certain amount of stone-building in London, which had been devastated by fire in 1135. In 1189 by the Assize of FitzAlwin, persons who built in stone and tile were given special privileges because their houses were so much less likely to catch fire. The same assize shows that some houses in London had party walls built of freestone, 3 ft. thick and 16 ft. high. From the top of the wall the roof, whether tiled or thatched, sloped down, and the gable end of the house faced the street. Thus, even if fire seized on and demolished the house itself, the party wall would almost certainly stand and with some little restoration, would again serve to hold a new construction.

What records are extant today show the early medieval home primarily as a shelter, a place for eating and sleeping and a workshop. Furnishing, even in the best homes, was simple. While one might sit on a stool or bench and lie at night on a wooden frame overlaid with straw, the nearest approach to man's modern favourite reclining posture was to squat on the floor with one's back against a wall. In the smaller houses life was even more spartan. Where the total home equipment was a table, a form, a few small stools, a cooking pot, a tripod and a gridiron; where double doors fitted badly, letting in draughts which blew acrid smoke in eddies about the room, home was rather a place to repair to in bad weather or when hungry or tired than to abide in during the day. He would have been a fool who wasted his time indoors when there was so much to do on a sunny, windy or frosty day outside.

As the centuries passed, increased amenities and comfort began to make the home a more attractive place. The improvement started, as was natural, among the upper classes and gradually crept down the social scale. The advent of the chimney made possible the complete rearrangement of interiors. Glass, which had been used in churches in Saxon times, was gradually taking the place of oiled silk and horn, though it was so dear that often only half a window was glazed while the other half was shuttered. In the fifteenth century it was no uncommon thing for persons to leave their windows in their wills, but in 1579 it was decided that by law, glass fixed by nails or in any other way to windows could not be moved, "for without glass is no perfect house". It was not, however, until the end of the eighteenth century that most cottages had glass windows.

In these and many other ways the English gentleman of the late Middle Ages brought comfort into his home. Tapestry and painted cloths had long been used to insulate rooms and to cover up damp in stone walls. Now the richer and more ambitious man lined his rooms with wainscot, covered his doors with curtains and screened off aisles and passages. The hard wooden benches of his forefathers were supplanted by settles whose backs gave support and kept out the draughts. Fixed (dormant) refectory tables, round tables and folding tables took the place of the old trestles. His bed, a wide wooden box into which his thick mattress fitted, was hung at the head and down the sides with curtains. The stool of his forefathers he had replaced with a wooden-backed chair. On a church misericord at Scriveton in Nottinghamshire we see him, clad in gown and hood, sitting in such a chair warming his feet before a roaring fire, while behind him a jug stands on a stool. The very names for all these new features, chair, chamber, tester, tapestry, cushion, suggest that they first appeared in the houses of those who used Norman French, that is, the upper classes. The peasantry, however, were not unaffected. The illustration suggests that even in the late Middle Ages there must have been many a peasant's cote which had its master's chair. And, though in the twelfth century the great majority of householders had no more than one room, in the fifteenth there were few houses with less than two, and the number of two-storeyed dwellings was increasing fast.

As yet the most common and most adaptable building material was wood, and the early centuries after the Norman conquest showed widespread development in cruck construction. Small cottages which show it in its simplest form are numerous. At Hepworth near Huddersfield is one which originally consisted of one narrow bay of only 13 ft. between the two crucks, crossing at the top. The whole framework probably rested on wooden sills laid on the ground wall. The under side of the existing tiebeam is grooved as if at one time upright stakes had been wedged in it to form the framework of the wattle and daub overlay, while a rounded piece cut out of the middle of the tiebeam made room for the top of a door. The area covered by the original roof was only about 13 ft. by 23 ft., but in the seventeenth century the cottage was enlarged by the building of a second room of stone, and the making of a five-foot extension beyond the crucks of the original framework and the addition of a new door off the centre. A second cottage at Hepworth enclosed an even smaller bay of 10 ft. In this the crucks, instead of crossing at the apex, met and were secured by a short collar beam. In other cottages there were two collar beams, sometimes strengthened by being notched into the crucks. Whereas at first the spaces between the vertical studs of the side and end walls were probably filled in entirely with wattle and daub, stone and bricks came to be used in later ages. In some cases the stone or bricks were built up to cover the crucks completely so that the original construction was not discovered until the cottage or barn was taken down or renovated. In others the surface of the crucks still remains, its outline standing out boldly against the surrounding stone, brick or plaster.

It is not known why cruck construction was never used in south-eastern counties and East Anglia. One writer suggests that the more advanced people of the south-east were architecturally more sensitive than the ruder inhabitants of the north and west and "would never have tolerated so unsightly a form of construction". It is unlikely, however, that the cottage-dweller anywhere had developed so fine a taste in building. Other suggestions were that the trees in the west and north were more suitable. This seems unlikely in view of the fact that some of the cruck-framed buildings are in areas not conspicuously well wooded, while in others known to have had dense oak forests in the Middle Ages they are entirely absent. The most likely explanation is that the south and south-east were always more open to influences from Continental countries such as France, the Netherlands and the Rhineland, which had no cruck houses.

Even in districts where these predominated there are striking differences. The least developed constructions are in the north, where builders were content if they obtained a lightly curving beam whose curve made the arc of a circle and which could be worked in the same thickness all along its length. This means that the bottom part of the cruck rises at an angle from the plinth or ground sill, thus affording less headroom. For the building of an outside wall, therefore, the tie-beam had to be extended well beyond the curve of the cruck before it reached a point directly over the base. In one instance, that of Leuth-waite Hall Barn, the stud which carries the end of the wall rises out of the cruck, thus increasing the headroom near the wall.

Only in one instance is the curve of the cruck angular, and this gives us an idea as to how the crucks were obtained. In this barn at Snowgate Head, New Mill, near Huddersfield, the crucks rise obliquely in a straight line then turn suddenly inwards two-thirds of the way up to meet at the apex where they are about half as thick as at the foot. This suggests that the top part of the cruck, when it was in the living tree, ran along a branch, and the foot was taken from well down the trunk.

The cruck-building region of England runs in a broad arc from Monmouthshire to Yorkshire and its mid point is in Herefordshire. Here, today, stands a collection of cottages mainly in the district around Weobley, unequalled in England and far more advanced in construction than those in Yorkshire. In the first place, whereas in the Huddersfield example the branch part of the cruck is at the apex, in all the counties from Herefordshire southwards, the tree is, as it were, turned upside down, the end which was the branch standing on the plinth.

On examination this position has many advantages. In the first place, the angle, which falls lower down the blade, allows the bottom part to stand almost vertically upright, so that the tiebeams hardly have to project at all, and the wall studs fit almost naturally into place between sill and wallplate. The wall is thus drawn nearer to the cruck blade, which is protected from exterior damp by one of the vertical studs and held in place by the tie-beam on which the wall plate is laid. At intervals along the length of the bay other vertical studs connect sill and wallplate. The rigidity of the cruck trusses is further increased by the purlins which run from one to the other and support the roof rafters. So strong was the whole construction that if the slender feet of the crucks should rot away, the half-timbered wall was enough to support the wall-plate and take the whole weight of the roof. In later days it was not uncommon, in the southern part of the region at least, to build stout walls of stone to the height of the doorway and place the crucks on them to gain five to six feet on the height of the building.

The medieval carpenter was a first-rate craftsman. His principal tool was the axe, which he used in many forms for a variety of jobs. The broad axe and the adze bit into and shaped the great beams; to make grooves, tenons and mortises he used the twybylle, a chisel-pointed pickaxe with two cutting edges, one in line with the handle, the other at right angles to it. Piercers and augers were used to bore holes, and the thickness of the timber was measured with a gauge called a skantyllyon, a word from which we derive the modern term scantling. The early carpenters despised the saw, but when it came to dividing the long curved trunks to make symmetrical crucks, there was no other possible tool.

Prefabrication was the general rule. The trees from which the main timbers were to be made had necessarily to be fairly close to one another in their growing state, for it was more convenient to shape them before they were carried to the building site, and no doubt there was much thought and argument about the choosing of them. Once the choice had been made, the work began. Ground was cleared and the small timbers sorted and shaped for studding, while the larger ones were felled and trimmed with the axe for collar-beams, tie-beams, purlins and rafters. A sawpit was dug, and the workers, taking turns, sweated and strained at the two-handed saw, one above and one underneath the great cruck-shaped beams. In this way every necessary part of the construction was prepared and marked. Then when all was ready the framework was carried in pieces to the site where already the stone footings or stylobats had been laid and mortared into place.

To make it easier to lift them, the crucks were often pierced at or near the feet with holes through which stout beams were passed, and the whole manhood of the village set to work, several on each side grasping the beams to ease the cruck on to its plinth, while others with ropes steadied it as it was being shifted into place. When the framework of the house was based and the ridge pole secure, the whole community "footed", or fêted, it with drinks and feasting all round. From that time on, the master of the new house could be safely left to carry on the fixing of the minor supports in the framework. In this state it looked rather like a gigantic cage, and the last stage was to clothe the skeleton by filling the interstices between the studding with wattle and daub, and by making the crossed framework on the roof on which the cover, generally some sort of thatch, was to be laid.

Though some writers dismissed cruck building as less handsome than the box-frame construction of the south and east, it had its own homely charm. Even today there is something very pleasing to the eye in the gentle sweep of a couple of stout boomerang-shaped timbers standing out against the later brick or plaster casing they were designed to support. Moreover, the cruck had the advantage that it could be used by both lord and vassal alike, because it was adaptable for the smallest cottage and limited for the building of larger halls only by the size of the locally grown timbers.

It is believed that the cruck type of construction was brought to England at an early date from the northern part of Germany and southern Denmark, probably by Danish immigrants, and that it spread by way of the Humber into the West Riding of Yorkshire, where before the Norman conquest the population was largely Anglo-Danish. Hogback tombstones of the late ninth and tenth centuries which are of cruck form seem to indicate that by 1066 the majority of buildings in this part of the country were on this principle. In 1069 William the Conqueror, because of resistance in the north, laid waste large areas of West Yorkshire. The entries in Domesday (1086) which gave the laconic entry "*vastata est*" ("It has been laid waste") show where this devastation took place. One of the districts spared lay immediately around Huddersfield, and here the cruck-trussed building form persisted. Elsewhere, as new inhabitants moved in, probably from a southerly direction, they brought with them the box-frame construction.

While on her way to church at Dewsbury on Christmas morning in the year 1261, Lady Heton, wife of the Lord of the Manor of Mirfield, was waylaid and robbed and her maid murdered. Later in the day, while she was at dinner, Lady Heton was visited by two begging friars who asked for alms to help them on their journey to Rome. Since her husband, Sir John, was at that time himself in Rome, this was an opportunity to send him news of her fortunate escape and through him to ask the Pope to spare the people of Mirfield the risk of making such journeys by elevating the chapel of ease there to a parish church. This was eventually done and a rectory was built in about the year 1300 by the younger brother of Sir

John who had been given the living. This is believed to have been one of the earliest frame-trussed buildings in the district.

The principle of construction is simple. Like the cruck-framed house, the unit is the bay, raised in the usual way on a ground sill resting on a plinth of stone, rubble or later, brick. At the four corners of the bay stand the wall posts bound together length-wise by the ground sill below and the wall plate above, and breadthwise by ground sill and tie-beam, which rests on the wall plate. This gives us a skeleton of twelve beams enclosing a space which is almost a cube. Into this cube are fitted the other beams which strengthen and complete the structure. Approximately half-way along all four sides of the cube, mortised into the posts, run the four breast-summers or bressumers, and at points where wall-posts meet horizontal beams (tie-beam, wall-plate and bressumers) the structure is made firmer by curved pieces called wind-braces.

The roof framework consists of two main rafters rising at each end to support the ridge pole, from which other rafters placed at regular intervals run down and are fastened on to the wall-plate. To support these, other beams called purlins, sometimes one, sometimes two on each side of the roof, run across from one main rafter to the other. All these beams, especially the ground sills, wall posts and wall plates and tie beams, were of considerable thickness and skilfully joined together so that the box frame could support a heavy roof covering of thatch or tile. The additional support needed for a large house was provided by adding wind braces, collar-beams and purlins on roof and walls. The roof of a smaller building might be secured by no more than collar beam and side purlins, but in others, especially buildings of more than one bay, posts were fixed on to the tie beams to hold up the collar-beams. The best known of these is the king-post, which rising from the middle of the tie-beam, supports either the ridge pole itself or a central purlin across which the collar-beams are placed to hold up the pairs of rafters.

Later, in about the fifteenth century, this was largely super-

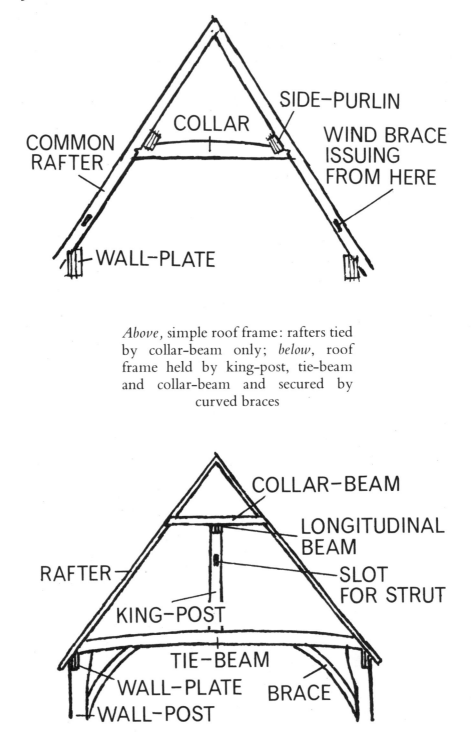

Above, simple roof frame: rafters tied by collar-beam only; below, roof frame held by king-post, tie-beam and collar-beam and secured by curved braces

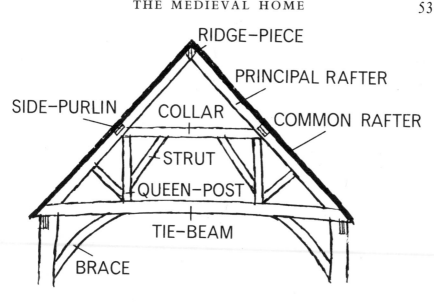

Roof with two queen-posts supporting collar-beam and rafter strengthened by braces

seded by a pair of queen-posts supporting the collar-beam at or near the ends, the whole construction made rigid by struts running from queen-posts to main-rafter and from queen-post to collar-beam.

The problem in all housebuilding is that of making extra rooms. The house into which a newly-married couple moved might in ten years or more be too small for a growing family, or an increase in prosperity might make its owner wish to add more rooms to it. Among ancient peoples who used the circular kind of dwelling this could be done only by building more small circular huts and enclosing these with a fence. In the cruck-frame construction there were two ways of extension— upwards into a chamber overhead or lengthwise by adding another bay or an outshut, though barns and larger houses were sometimes widened by putting in long tie-beams and creating a kind of aisle along the length of the building, so that the walls and roof entirely enclosed the crucks and formed outshuts beyond them. In other cases these outshuts were made

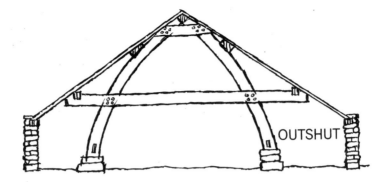

Section of building showing cruck
construction widely extended

by complicated patterns of beams placed outside the crucks
and supporting an extended roof. This, however was uncommon in smaller houses where the usual way was to extend
lengthwise beyond the crucks. Thus the house came to have
two parts, one known as the house-part, the original building,
and the rest being the additions, the larders and chambers
around or above it.

The way such a house grew from its beginnings as a cruck-
framed cottage may be seen in buildings which are still existing. First we have the single bay, roof thatched, walls of wattle
and daub on a timber framing, the fire in the middle of the
house-part and smoke escaping through a hole in the roof.
Later this came to be extended by a large jutty or lean-to at
one end, and this, connected by a door to the house-part became the chamber or even two chambers. On the other end of
the building a second small extension, possibly without windows or entrances for light, was used as a larder and storage
place, commonly known as the buttery (derived from the
word butt and having no connection with butter).

A cruck-framed cottage could always be extended by building on to it one or more bays, but since the bay was one of the
units of taxation, it was far cheaper as well as easier to add
outshuts instead. The thatch needed only to be extended in one

or two places until it covered the whole building like a large bonnet.

The occupant could be protected from draughts coming through the doorway either by a small porch on the outside or a screen on the inside called a speer. While the fire was in the centre of the large room, the use of the roofspace as an upper chamber was not very feasible, for it was there that the smoke collected before finding its way out through a louvre at the apex of the roof. When, however, the hearth was moved to a side wall, the creation of an upper storey was made easier. In the house-part, on the side opposite to the fireplace, the cottager might make a hay-loft by laying horizontal beams at a height of six to seven feet and laying planks over them. This could be left open for storage or closed up with boards and a small door and, reached by a ladder, would serve as a small bedchamber. The position of the fire, laid against a reredos in front of a wall, made it easier to catch the smoke in a large inverted funnel or hood made of wood and plaster. This and the chimney-breast below it often extended as far as four or five feet into the room. The canopy extended into the chamber above, sloping upwards towards the louvre, taking up a large part of the upper room and spreading the warmth of the fire into it. This, the "room in the chimney", was the warmest and cosiest bedchamber in the house.

Even in the most advanced of these small houses, living by modern standards was extremely comfortless and rough. Though roof-hole or louvre drew out some of the smoke there was always a great deal, especially on gusty days, floating about inside, wafted here and there by the continuous draughts from chinks in the shuttered "wind-eyes" and ill-fitting door of planks hanging on its pin-hook hinges. The poor widow of Chaucer's Nonne Priestes Tale lived in such a simple cottage, its two mean rooms blackened by years of fire-smoke:

"Ful sooty was hir bour and eek hir halle"
In one corner of her hall a perch stretched from wall to wall,

and on it sat the widow's handsome and prized cockerel Chauntecleer, whose crowing was as regular and melodious as the bell in the abbey tower. Ranged alongside him, shuffling their feathers, were his seven hens who added to the melody. These were probably not the only animal inhabitants, for we read that in her yard, which was

"enclosed all aboute
With stikkes and a drye dich with-oute"

were three large sows, three cows and a sheep called Malle.

The simple diet of the peasant needed no elaborate cooking; the fire and a couple of iron pots serving all his needs. The poor peasant woman ate so little that she was never in danger of taking an apoplectic fit, her diet being mainly "white and black", i.e. milk and coarse bread with the occasional relief of a morsel of boiled bacon or an egg or two. Of the modern amenities there were none. Her bed was probably a pallet stuffed with straw, laid out on the floor or a low wooden frame. Toilets and baths were non-existent. A single rough chest was enough to contain all one family's personal belongings. Yet the conditions that had existed in pre-Roman times still held good in the medieval village. The house of a peasant was as yet little more than a shelter and a retreat. The need to make a living probably forced even the poor widow and her two daughters to spend most of their time out in the open in the small toft on the fields or the village, returning indoors only to rest and sleep.

Before the fourteenth century the majority of the inhabitants of England lived in the country, and of these the wealthy were far outnumbered by the poor. These, the humble shepherd, ploughman and the village craftsman, were the backbone of England's wealth in peacetime and the source of her might in war. Poems and chronicles tell us much about their outlook on life, and new light is constantly being shed on their social conditions, their standard of living and industries, but on one subject, the actual form and appearance of the houses they lived in, we are left, because of the absence of evidence, to make no more than a pretty confident assumption.

As we have seen, there are three main patterns, the first the straight or curved rafters from ground to ridge-tree either with or without basing-stones or plinths; the second the box-frame construction, both these finished by some form of wattle and daub, and the third, the frameless building made by piling stone on stone or rearing thick walls of rammed earth. But whatever the pattern of building, the form remained the same, beginning with the construction of a single room or bay, and its elaboration either by throwing out either more bays or outshuts, or building upwards.

By the end of the fifteenth century England stood on the verge of vast changes. By this time it is believed that even the poor had dwellings of at least two rooms. Chaucer (d. 1400) talks of the widow's house and bower—two separate rooms, while in different parts of the country other words appear. In the south the bower becomes the ground-floor room known as the parlour (French *parler*–to talk), a word taken from medieval monastic life, while in the north it is called the chamber. Later both words came to be used generally with different meanings. Thus from the hovel, finally emerged the cottage.

IV

Half Timber

"The English," said a Spanish visitor in the time of Queen Mary I, "have their houses made of sticks and dirt, but they fare commonly as well as a king."

When he marvelled that such good fare could be set out in the "coarse cabins" in which the English lived, he had in mind the homely cottages of the common people, but many fifteenth-century manor houses were also composed of "sticks and dirt".

Medieval England, as so many of its place-names tell us, was rich in forests. It was the forest that produced the great oak beams of the Saxon hall and barn, and the same tradition of building was followed in the construction of the fourteenth-century timber-framed country house. In it, the hall remained, its steeply pitched roof held up by stout pillars sloping down to low eaves, and making the aisles, so familiar in Saxon days. The fire still burned in the centre of the hall, and the smoke escaped through a hole in the roof. The dais at which the master and his family dined occupied one end of the enormous room.

But in the course of centuries the old type of hall had been modified by additions in an entirely different style. The desire for increased comfort had called for the building of parlours and solars at the master's end of the hall, and the desire for more convenient service had required the addition of the buttery and pantry at the other end. Yet the two styles—the one-storey Saxon hall open to the roof, and the two-storey box-frame wings came to be blended, so as to produce an H-shaped building of pleasing appearance, with a door, not now in the end, but in the side of the main hall at the farther end from the master's dais, while the hall was protected from draughts by screens which made a sort of passage. Behind the dais was the parlour for the master and his family, with perhaps a store. Above this was the solar, or best chamber. The word comes from the Latin *solarium*, which was a room built at the top of a Roman building, looking towards the south, in which people could bask in the sun (*sol*–the sun). England cannot boast of having as much sun as Italy, but the country gentlemen gave this name to his best and lightest room. At the other end of the building, behind the passage covering the entry doors, were the service rooms and pantry, sometimes with a narrow passage between them, leading into the hall from an outside kitchen.

In the fifteenth century great changes gradually crept over the face of England. Of these the first was political. The long, drawn-out war with France, in spite of the glories of Crecy, Poitiers and Agincourt, ended in a series of disasters which brought about the almost complete expulsion of the English from their French dominions. But the wars had raised up in England itself a body of gentlemen who had been accustomed to live on the fruits of war, and a proud and arrogant nobility whose members saw no way of life other than wasting their substance and even their lives in bitter struggles for self-advancement under the banners of Lancaster or York. Thus the Wars of the Roses ended in the almost complete extinction of the old nobility.

While all this was happening, other social classes were quietly advancing in wealth and influence. In the countryside the old custom of holding land by feudal tenure was giving way to the payment of money rents, and landlords seeking the freedom from responsibility that only money could give, were disposing of their lands by sale and lease. The buyers and lessees were the new class of thrifty and enterprising farmers whose ancestors may have been villeins or even serfs but who now were accumulating money, hedging in their small estates, enlarging them by the exchange of the strips they had held in the common fields and by taking in surrounding plots of waste to create larger farms under private ownership. While some continued to raise crops, others turned their attention from agriculture to sheep-farming. In this way arose a new class of middling and prosperous farmers known as yeomen. Meanwhile, in spite of civil war, foreign and internal trade was brisk and in the towns the merchant class was growing in numbers and affluence. Many of these merchants, having made money in trade, invested it in country estates and joined the yeoman class in the exploitation of the land.

All this had its effect on the construction and appearance of the English home. England came to be dotted with houses which were simpler and smaller versions of the great hall of the manorial lord. The central hall, which in the larger house had its screens, dais and passages, would in the smaller house be no more than one large room and kitchen combined and, having less roof space, could be built without aisles. This the yeoman, his family and his labourers would use as a dining- and common-room. The private part of the yeoman's house

Medieval interior with oak framework; Colliers Hatch, near North Weald, Essex

Typical oak studding in a medieval cottage; *below*, medieval English cottage with later extensions, chimneys and weatherboarding; Colliers Hatch, Essex

would be the family parlour at one end, above which was the bedchamber. Stores and implements would be kept either in an adjoining room or shed, at the other end, or in one of the nearby outhouses. This practice of the master, his family and employees living much of their lives as one closely-knit unit was typically English, praised by such writers as Cobbett and continued in some country districts up to the present day.

Apart from the primitive peasant's hovel, the development of the English house stems from the medieval aisled hall, which underwent changes in certain directions to suit differing requirements. The first was the disappearance of the aisles in the smaller yeoman's house, the second was the enlargement of the upper storey in the box-frame additions at the ends and the third was the insertion of an upper storey in the central hall itself, which tended to diminish the importance of this part of the building altogether and in time to convert it, upstairs and downstairs, into a number of separate rooms. Of all these developments the most interesting and easiest to see in old houses is the second, known as jettying.

Several explanations have been given for the projecting

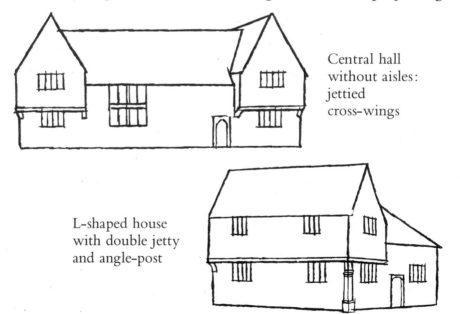

Central hall
without aisles:
jettied
cross-wings

L-shaped house
with double jetty
and angle-post

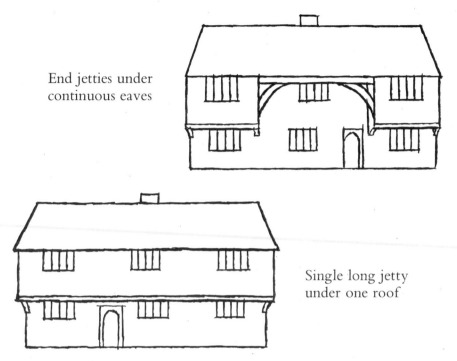

End jetties under
continuous eaves

Single long jetty
under one roof

upper storey of the medieval house. S. O. Addy suggests that
these features, which give beauty to so many old English
towns were added purposely to give shelter to the owners of
stalls and booths underneath, and that, though there was no
real use for them in country houses, the fashion of building
them spread. It is true that the shelter given by the overhang
was a boon both to trader and passer-by. In past centuries when
young bloods met in the street they often fell to fighting as to
who should "take the wall", and even today it is usual for the
man to yield this place to the lady. But this, if it is one explanation, is not the only one. Another which has as much to justify
it, and which applies to both the town and country house, is
that the projecting upper storey helped to keep the damp from
the ground sills. This was very important in days when there
were no such things as gutters, fall pipes or damp courses, for
the constant flowing of water down exterior walls would tend
to soften the infilling between the studs, carrying the damp
into the lower parts of the house.

The most likely explanation is that this projecting upper storey added to the stability of the house and the comfort of the people in it. Imagine, for instance, that it was desired to add a first floor to an existing one-storey building, a thing which must often have been done. This involved first, framing up this storey which, when prepared, would be placed on top of the lower one after the roof had been taken off. The support for this would be the floor joists laid parallel to each other, and resting on the walls of the ground floor. The floor joists of today are oblong in section, and, since they rest on their shorter sides, offer the maximum resistance to weights laid on them. This, however, was not always the case. The medieval floor joists could be square in section, or, if oblong, were generally laid on their longer sides. In either case the floor of an upper storey was certain to sag a little when weight was placed on it, and this sag would increase with the passing of years. The medieval builder knew this, and to minimise the sag made the floor joists of the upper storey overhang the walls below, and then erected the walls of the upper storey on the ends of the joists. The weight of these upper walls tended to force up the joists at their middles, thus neutralising the sag and bringing the floor more level. This rough and ready method of making one force counterbalance another was very successful. It had the extra advantage of providing more floor space in the upper storey, something which was very badly needed in towns where buildings tended to be closely packed together.

Whereas at first jettying could be carried out only on one side wall or on two opposite sides of a building, a later dis-covery made it possible for an upper storey to project on adjacent sides, or even on all four sides. This was the insertion into a post in the centre of the building, of a strong beam called the dragon beam which stretched out diagonally to the corner of the projection and was supported near its outer end by another heavy angle-post. This post was usually cut from the complete trunk of a tree, inverted so that the thicker end

Close studding and angle-posts. A Tudor cottage in King Street, Margate, Kent

had a large enough area to support the whole corner at the junction. Into the dragon-beam were framed the joists which met it at right angles one to another. The angle-beams which supported the structure were sometimes elegantly carved and may still be seen at the exterior corners of timber-framed houses. In many, especially in Cheshire, the joists are supported at the overhang by braces, curved and fitted into the junction with upright studs.

Jettying had a profound effect on the aspect of the house both in town and country. In the towns, where space was limited, the natural tendency was to build upwards, and with every storey added, the houses on opposite sides of the street approached nearer and nearer to each other, until it became possible in some places for neighbours to shake hands across the street. This helped to give the medieval town its peculiar atmosphere of bustle and industry, but added considerably to its dangers. The almost closed character of the street prevented the entry of light and air and when, as was almost universally the case, drainage was by means of an open gutter or kennel running down the middle, smells and putrefaction bred disease. Where, too, a craftsman carried on his work at the place in which he lived, selling his wares at the open shop front, the noise of hammer and saw, added to the smells of dye, entrails and tallow, tended to increase the discomfort. The effects of such conditions were lessened to some extent in that, unlike today, no townsman was in any place more than a few minutes' walk from the open country, but there was one danger from which he had little protection, that of fire. When an outbreak occurred, especially if there was any wind, the streets were air-funnels which carried the fire and spread it far and wide.

The invasion of the town, first by horse-drawn traffic and more recently by the motor vehicle, led to a complete change or perversion of the true function of a street, and there is every sign that the town planner of today with his idea of the shopping precinct is returning to the medieval idea, for the medieval main street was a shopping precinct pure and simple and was for the use mainly of people who went on foot. "It was made," said Sir William Davenant, "in the days of wheel-barrows, before these greater engines, carts, were invented." The horse-drawn vehicle, indeed anything taking up more room than a loaded ass, was an intrusion. John Lydgate, (c. 1370-1451), in his poem *London Lickpenny*, describes how all the way from Cheapside in London to Eastcheap near the Tower was one continuous street market:

> *Then went I forth by London Stone*
> *Throughout all Can'wick Street.*
> *Drapers much cloth me offered anon;*
> *Then comes me one cried, 'Hot sheep's feet!'*
> *One criede 'Mackerel!' 'Rushes green!' another*
> *gan greet;*
> *One bade me buy a hood to cover my head,*
> *But for want of money I might not be sped.*

Then I hied me into East Cheap;
One cries 'Ribs of beef,' and many a pie;
Pewter pottes they clatter'd on a heap,
There was harpe, pipe and minstrelsie.
'Yea, by cock!' 'Nay by cock!' some began to cry;
Some sung of Jenkin and Julian for their meed,
But for lack of money I might not speed.

In these narrow streets the traders laid out their goods on their open stalls or shop fronts and set their touts or apprentices to bring in customers. To them the narrow street was an advantage, and they did all they could to make it even narrower. Some pushed out the fronts of their premises, making "jutties", others dug cellars and semi-basements beneath their houses which were entered by stairs going down from street level. These basements, called taverns, from the Latin *taberna*, meaning a booth or a hut, were also used as shops, but because they were underground and on that account could be hidden from public gaze, they tended to attract the wine and liquor trade. Thus the name tavern came to be associated with drinking on the premises. The entries to these taverns further restricted the amount of room in the streets and some towns collected annual rents for such encroachments from their owners. When, round about the year 1600, the traffic problem became really serious, royal proclamations had to be issued to stop further development of "that noisome peste of Bulkes, Stalls, Shedds, Carts and Juttyes."

From reading poems, chronicles and accounts we can imagine what street life was like in the Middle Ages. To the townsman the street was not only his shopping centre; it was his newsroom where he took in the latest reports and gossip, the club where he met his cronies, his place of entertainment when the crafts performed their miracle and morality plays, where penitents walked in hair shirts carrying lighted candles, where offenders were drawn on hurdles over the uneven cobbles or stood in the pillory. It was the place of pageantry when the gilds or the city fathers made progresses to their saint's chapel or some important personage visited the town. The street, in fair weather or foul, was much more of a home than the miserable place in which he spent his nights.

There is little to tell us what these dwellings of the town poor were like. Though the space within the walls was restricted, the whole area was not necessarily built up. William Langland (*c.* 1330–1400) in his *Vision of Piers Plowman* tells us that he lived with his wife and daughter in a hovel in Cornhill (near to where the present Royal Exchange now stands). Also even within the town walls there were often monasteries with their gardens, and the richer citizens too had houses set in their own land, with winding paths and pleasant arbours. Town populations were small, and by the fourteenth century building had already begun outside the walls of most of the fortified towns. Town life presents us with a picture of great contrasts between the very rich and the very poor, and between gracious living which existed side by side with over-crowding, disease and vice.

In the poorer parts of a medieval town, the dwellings were huddled together with no sort of plan. Many stood away from the main streets in little courts, either closed altogether save for the entry or connected by narrow alleys. Living in a court had certain advantages. Since no traffic passed through, it was cleaner underfoot and much freer from outside intrusion than the street. It was therefore a kind of miniature closed-in village consisting of families all well-known to each other. Some sort of community spirit and mutual help was therefore possible. But it cannot be assumed that the inhabitants lived one family to one house, for the limitation of ground space in the industrial parts of a town or near the busy quays of a river would not allow of it. From Roman times, the apartment or tenement had been a common feature of town life. Large numbers of the Roman poor had lived in such quarters, which were usually in blocks called *insulae*, put up by speculative builders, with few conveniences and, often being jerry-built, subject to sudden collapse or fire.

Since timber was still the only material out of which the frames of houses were made, these tenements were box-framed, three or even four storeys high and greatly over-crowded. With the limitations of imperfect water-supply and primitive methods of sanitation, the proper cleanliness of home and person were alike impossible, and one cannot by the farthest stretch of the imagination picture the dreadful conditions under which townspeople of the poorer sort must have lived. The high rate of mortality, especially among the young, and the ravages of plague and other diseases, infectious and contagious, is not to be wondered at.

Between the very poor and the very wealthy came the self-employed craftsmen, respectable and respected members of their gilds, each keeping in his house, besides his family, the number of apprentices sanctioned by his gild. Their homes generally lined the main streets of the town, each occupation living in its own special quarter, remembered even today by the names of its streets, as in London. The craftsman's stall and workshop were usually in front of the building, on the ground floor, and behind them was the living-room. In the twelfth century most of these houses were probably of two storeys only, the upper room projecting over the shop front. Later, as the owner became more affluent, his house came to be extended, upwards by means of a garret and downwards with a cellar. Now the uses of the rooms came to be more special-ised. The ground-floor room behind the shop became the general room for family, journeymen and apprentices, where all ate during the day and where household jobs were done. In this sense it corresponded to the hall in the yeoman's house, while the first-floor solar became the private room and chief living room of the family. Even today the shopkeeper, especially in the provincial towns of England, has his front room directly over his shop.

The extension upwards was given the name *garret*, originally a military term meaning a watch-tower (Old French *garite*), and this room, often built up partly into the roof space, made a second projection bringing the house nearer to the one across the street. It was used as a bedroom, generally for servants and apprentices. The cellar furnished extra storage, and in some houses, especially those crowded close together with little or no garden space, a part of it was dug extra deep and served as a cesspool. Pits of this kind were not only dangerous to health: later, when the earth became saturated with sewage from the cesspools and seeped into the wells and underground watercourses, London and some provincial towns had serious problems of water supply and drainage.

Improvements in the construction of timber-framed houses, which made possible these developments in towns, also brought infinite variety to the new buildings being raised during the fifteenth century in the country. New manor-houses arose in which the roof of the central hall was heightened and the cross-wings jettied, giving much unity of style to the building. By this time people were beginning to appreciate the value of brick. By using it in chimneys it became possible to remove the hearth from the centre of the hall to one wall. This satisfied those families who were changing their sleeping habits and wanted more privacy, therefore more small rooms. These could now be made. The vacant space high in the interior of the central hall could be utilised by the construction of a second storey within the hall itself. The next tendency was therefore for the cross-wings to disappear altogether as separate parts of the building and to remain only as jettied upper rooms at the two ends, the whole being brought under one roof, the windows aligned. The central hall, instead of being the great high room it once was almost disappeared, this space between the two jetties being narrowed and heightened to contain the two storeys. Now what was left of the hall was no more than a large room with chambers above it, the overhanging roof supported by two huge curved braces. Thus solar, hall, buttery, chambers and stores were brought together. The old manorial hall had given way to the new country house. It was but a step from this to the building of a house under one roof with one continuous jetty, three windows in line on the ground floor, three on the first floor and one chimney serving the middle part of the house.

With a second storey and the possibility of all-round jetty-ing, houses of many shapes and sizes could be built. In towns, where they often had to be fitted into plots of land of irregular shapes and limited area, these building improvements came in extremely useful. In these irregularly-shaped houses the hall continued to lose its importance as the general place of assembly and functioned simply as the main living-room for the family; the variety in building was mainly in the wings. Thus between the fourteenth and sixteenth centuries, large numbers of L-shaped and T-shaped houses were built, the main doors of all of them being in the usual place, just by the projection.

Wherever it could be obtained, oak was the best material for the frames of houses, and heart of oak for pegs or dowels which bound together the various parts of the frames. But since oak takes a long time to dry out and season, it was customary to fell the tree, trim it and use it within a very short time.

The felling was done with the broad axe, and if the trunk was extra thick, its heart was worked through with a narrow axe and the trunk was split by knocking in wedges with the axe, or later, with the three-handed hammer called a beetle. The beams and studs were then cut by two-handed saws and, though the plane was in use in the fifteenth century, they were usually trimmed with the adze, which for hard wood on which a smooth surface was not required, was efficient enough and much speedier. When all was prepared, complete with tenons and mortises and holes marked for dowels, the various main sections were fixed together, numbered with Roman numerals, then dismantled and taken to the site. Here

"Wood, unlike steel or stone, is never still." A study in angles, Lavenham, Suffolk

they were framed up and all the menfolk in the locality joined in the job of "rearing" and hammering in the pegs to fit them together.

Once the house had been built the wood still had to go through the drying-out and maturing process. In time this affected the whole building, giving the characteristic lurch and sagging of the floorboards of a medieval house. In addition, wood, even oak, unlike steel or stone, is never still. Wet weather brings expansion, dry weather contraction. Straight timbers show curvatures, plaster falls out and has to be renewed. All this, combined with a three- or four-storey overhang, gave to certain houses a very unsteady appearance and the impression that they were liable to topple over at anytime.

If bressumers, tie-beams, wall-plates and angle-posts are counted as part of the construction, the earlier half-timber houses contained much more timber than any other material,

Square, decorated panels and ornamental braces; Moreton
Hall, Cheshire

Sixteenth-century half-timbered labourers' cottages,
heavily restored

and the filling-in between the studs was, in fact, a part of the
finishing process. But by the sixteenth century so much of the
country's timber had been used for making charcoal for gunpowder, the smelting of iron and the building of ships and
houses that supplies were beginning to run out. Thus in
earlier houses we usually find, especially in the south and east,
panels and studs alternating at equal distances. Essex, Suffolk
and Surrey can still produce excellent examples of close half-
timber with long vertical panels. In the north-west and west,
however, where the country was not quite so well forested,
there was more use of horizontal timbers, and a preference for
square panels decorated with patterns worked by shaping the
braces inserted in them. Here and in Yorkshire diagonal
studding is far more frequent. Gables are half-timbered,
sometimes with studs parallel to the rafters, sometimes at
right angles to them, and side walls have vertical timbers

studded with shorter ones in herring-bone patterns.

Where the studding of later timber houses is visible it often gives clear evidence of the need to use timber sparingly. The studs are much farther apart and some members, especially braces, are curved because straight ones were scarce and therefore expensive. Oak, which at first had been used exclusively, came to be supplemented by sweet chestnut which resembled it in appearance. Timbers of larger houses which had been demolished were put on one side to be cut up later and used in the construction of smaller houses. Such timbers were much more liable to warp even than the new wood, and this accounts for the irregularities, especially in the floorboards of some old cottages. It is not, therefore, a difficult matter to guess, from an examination of the shape and position of posts, studs and braces, the rough date at which a half-timbered house was constructed.

When the frame of the house had been erected, came the process of thatching and infilling. In London, owing to the danger of fire, thatch was replaced by tiles in the thirteenth century. In other parts of the country it remained in use. In the late nineteenth and early twentieth centuries, when slates and tiles were made and transported by the million, there was a danger that the thatcher's craft would go out of existence, but thanks to the motor-car and the recent influx of affluent townsmen to the countryside, it has regained in popularity and some handsome newly-thatched roofs may be seen, especially in the south and east.

The materials used for thatch depended largely on the locality in which one lived. Where marshes and saltings existed, reed was the most common, though the most difficult to use. It was easily obtainable on the banks of some slowly-flowing rivers like the Great Ouse, and indeed all over the Fens before they were drained, and on the salt marshes of Essex and Thames-side. No doubt the value of the reeds was one among many reasons why in some parishes on the north bank of the Thames the marshes were rated at a much higher figure than the agricultural and pastoral areas farther inland. In the Middle Ages, when the Essex saltings were populated by thousands of sheep and supplied cheese to London as Skelton tells us,

> *well a foot thicke*
> *Full of magots quicke.*
> *It was huge and great*
> *And mighty strong meat*
> *For the Devill to eat,*
> *It was tart and punicate.*

the rude marshmen's huts scattered about these marshes in places where nobody now lives, must have been thatched with reeds.

In places where reeds were hard to get, the material generally used was straw, especially wheat straw which had not been bruised or broken and was not likely to give entrance into a roof to the weather or to tempt the birds. In moorland regions, in northern Ireland and Scotland, heather was the easiest material to get. It was tough and not subject to rotting, though after a while in place it tended to turn black. Others were sedge (Cambridgeshire), flax (Derbyshire) and broom. Walter the Tyler led the peasants in their revolt of 1381, but compared with the thatcher's his was a comparatively new craft.

The need to economise in the use of timber made certain changes inevitable in the methods of infilling. The composition of wattle and daub depended entirely on the region in which the house was being built. Wattle (from the Old English *watel* a hurdle) could be of any pliable wood. The ancient Egyptians, who lived in a land with hardly any timber, made walls of wattle and daub, using for the uprights stems of maize, and woven between them, tough flexible osiers or withies, thus making a slender fence which was plastered thickly on both sides with mud to strengthen it. The English used willow, hazel or ash sticks and, for the best work, laths of riven oak which were both tough and pliable. There was no question of nailing, for nails were far too expensive for such work. In the oldest houses, grooves were made in the horizontal beams and into these the laths were sprung, vertically, then sometimes tied together or strengthened by the interweaving of cross-pieces. When the gaps between the uprights became wider, it was necessary to have a stronger framework of wattle, and this was made by springing stout sticks into grooves made in the sides of the studs, then tying or weaving in the upright wattles. Daub, or dab is a word which explains itself. The material was made with any suitable earth that was at hand, preferably clay, the stickier and more tenacious the better, toughened with cowhair or chopped straw and combined if possible with some lime to increase its hardening properties. For a day's daubing considerable quantities of this were needed, and it was handled by two men, one on the inside, the other on the outside, throwing it smartly on to the wattle at the same time, so that the daub keyed itself securely into the framework. In houses where the studs were close together they stood out in ridges on the finished wall above the infilling, but in houses of a later date, the thinner the studs and the wider the space between them to be filled, the stronger the filling needed. Thus studs and filling tended to form one level surface. Later still, when the ironfounders of the midlands began to produce nails in plenty, the laths were often nailed to the studs on the outside and uprights tied to them, sometimes with string, on the inside. From the interior of the house a thick layer of daub was laid on, and a thin layer on the outside. Since in this building the studs were no longer an exterior feature but were partly covered by nailed laths, the daub was thrown over them also, and a layer of plaster laid over the whole. Thus we have a timber-framed house with a plain wall and not a beam or timber showing.

A covering of plaster was very necessary for these houses owing to the expansion and contraction of the walls in heat and cold, and the disintegrating effects of damp on the daub outside. Plaster, which was made with lime, sand and cow-hair, was more resistant to extremes both of temperature and humidity, thus giving protection to the walls and preventing cracks, draughts and decay. From early times the plaster was washed over with some kind of colouring. Judging from illuminated manuscripts of the Middle Ages, the Anglo-Saxons used to colourwash their buildings. In the north of England and in Scotland limewash was tinted with a lichen dye known as "archil" which a dictionary of 1678 described as "archal, otherwise liverwort, because it groweth upon the freestones of the mountain Peak." It gave the walls a deep-blue colour. Other tints were obtained from ochre, umber, yellow clay and green copperas. The colouring of cottage walls has continued up to the present and been enthusiastically taken up by the bungalow-dweller who in these days of fast dyes may choose any colour he pleases.

Besides wattle and daub, various other materials such as clay lump (Suffolk), flint and clunch (Sussex), oak boarding (Kent), sandstone (Herefordshire) and slate (Lincolnshire) have been used for infilling, but all these are very rare. A more common material was brick. Probably the proportion of timbered houses with brick nogging is greater today than it was in the fifteenth century, for at that time bricks were expensive to make and heavy to transport. They also had certain grave disadvantages when combined with timber, for their weight tended to put a severe strain on the framework of a building, especially if they were not keyed to the timbers as they needed to be if they were to remain in place. Many medieval and Tudor house-builders therefore strove to get the best of both worlds by making the outer facings of their infilling with brick, while the interior was coated with wattle and daub and then plastered. Of all methods of laying the bricks the herringbone pattern was most popular, for besides exerting pressure on the studs which tended to keep the bricks in place, it was and still is attractive to the eye. Because of its firmness and durability, brick tended to replace wattle and daub when old houses came to be renovated, and there are many today which even in this century have been filled in with brick nogging.

V

Tudor Splendour and Squalor

The battle of Bosworth was fought on the 22nd August, 1485. As a political event it seemed no more important at the time than Wakefield or Barnet, when the tide had been turned by the deaths of king-makers, and not by any means as important as Tewkesbury, where the only surviving Lancastrian heir to the throne had lost his life. When the news of Bosworth reached the ears of the yeoman and peasant, they saw in it nothing more than another turn in the wheel of fortune in a tiresome war with which they were not concerned.

Very well, England had another new king. What of it?

It was not the event, but the results of the event which made history. Other battles had thinned the ranks of the nobility, and Bosworth completed the process. Luckily for England, Henry Tudor was in himself a strong enough character to deal with the few who were left alive. John de Vere, 13th Earl of Oxford, had fought by his side at Bosworth, but this did not save him later from being fined £10,000 for keeping armed retainers in contravention of the Statute of Liveries. This is but one instance which shows how Henry brought to England what no other man for a century had been able to bring – the gift of political peace.

The Tudor peace was by no means unbroken, but for more than a century royal authority was never seriously challenged, and it was in this atmosphere of peace that the developments which had begun in previous centuries came to full fruition. In this sense the Tudors acted as catalysts in a society which was rapidly changing, and in no aspect of life was anything more changed than the English home. Stow, describing London in the reign of Elizabeth I, never ceases to marvel and

Tudor splendour. Ornamental brick chimneys, a steep gable and patterns of tiles. Houses at Albury, Surrey

sometimes to lament the astonishing transformations that had taken place in the City during his lifetime. William Harrison, rector of Radwinter in Essex, could write in his *Description of England* (1577) about no less astonishing developments in country life where, in spite of monopolies and grants by which privileged people battened on the wealth of the community, "we do yet find the means to obtain and achieve such furniture as heretofore hath been impossible", and that old men in his village "have noted three things to be marvellously altered in England to their sound remembrance." These were "the multitude of chimneys lately erected", the increase of comfort in the bedroom, and the substitution of pewter and tin tableware for the old wooden platters and dishes. In addition he remarks how much better off the husbandman was in his day than in times which still remained in man's memory.

The changes had their roots in events long since past. The discovery that gunpowder could be used for throwing heavy missiles had put an end to the value of the castle as a means of defence or oppression, and it became as extinct as the old nobility it had once housed. The urge to trade with foreign lands brought about the establishment of chartered companies whose members drew rich profits, and it was further stimulated by the prospect of a share in the riches that were flowing into Europe as a result of the discovery of lands west of the Atlantic. El Dorado, the Land of Gold is a Spanish expression, but the English were no less eager to reach it. Fortunes which had been made in the City were invested in land and stock. Thus many a man whose father had been a city merchant ended by becoming a country gentleman and some even attained noble rank. For those who did not the King found abundant work in the capacity of Justices of the Peace, on whose shoulders he piled the whole burden of county administration, the upkeep of Quarter Sessions and the oversight of the affairs of all the parishes in their counties. All these "new men" needed houses, but since the country was at peace and walls were in any case useless against the new weapons, there was no need for elaborate fortification. Thus a new kind of country house came into being and the English countryside experienced a boom in building such as never before occurred.

With the coming of the new nobility and the idea of the country gentleman there developed the conception of the "gentle life". In 1477 Caxton had produced the first book ever to be printed in England, and the desire to read, or at least to have a library, was kindled in the mind of the gentry. Meanwhile in Italy the material for furnishing it was being produced in quantity. Here there had taken place a new movement of liberation from the medieval traditions in art, literature, science and music, and this had rapidly spread to other countries. Books were being written and translated, pictures and portraits were being painted on canvas to be hung on walls, and sculptures were being produced. The rich man became a collector, and needed a long gallery in his house to display his treasures. The old beamed hall was no longer good enough. He must have plaster on the inner walls, large windows of glass to let in the light, and Italian craftsmen must be hired to create and execute plaster designs on his ceilings. He delighted to give learned men hospitality in his home and employed them to educate his children. Among the gentry the womenfolk in particular benefited from this burst of intellectual life, and even excelled their menfolk in learning. Sir Anthony Cooke, of Gidea Hall in Romford, had four such accomplished daughters and his house, as one visitor said, was like a Tusculan villa, "except that in this Tusculum the industry of the females was in full vigour". His eldest daughter married Sir William Cecil, his second married Sir Nicholas Bacon and was the mother of the famous essayist, while his third married as her second husband John, Lord Russell.

The Elizabethan mansion on which many a successful or ambitious noble spent a large part of his fortune stands in a class by itself. It was a work of art with its formal garden and terraces, its wide square-headed windows and expansive two-storey bays, its great chamber capable of seating hundreds of guests, its walls lined with artistic treasures brought from all over the world, its turrets and battlements now rather objects of ornament than means of defence. Such a house was Audley End, built by the Earl of Suffolk, grandson of Sir Thomas Audley on the site of Saffron Walden Abbey, acquired by Sir Thomas as part of the spoils of the monasteries. The house, begun in 1603 and finished in 1611, cost at least £200,000, much of it raised by the most flagrant sale of offices. When King James visited it shortly after its completion, viewing its two great rectangular courts, its corridors supported on alabaster pillars, its ornate ceilings and elaborate staircases, he remarked sarcastically to his host that the house might well do for a Lord Treasurer but was far too ostentatious for a king.

Meanwhile, among the lower grades of society the order was changing. No more do we hear mention of freeman, villein, bordar and serf. The invasion of the land by the capitalist farmer had brought about an almost complete disruption of the old system, and had ushered in the yeoman.

The *yeman*, or villager, of Old England was both farmer and soldier. He appears in Chaucer's Canterbury Tales as the personal attendant of the young squire, clothed in coat and hood of green, bearing a stout longbow and a sheaf of arrows. He marched with Edward III, the Black Prince and Henry V in the French Wars, and then, if he was spared to return home, settled down in peace to till his land. In the great redistribution that took place throughout the fifteenth century the sons and grandsons of the yeomen, thrifty and far-seeing, increased their holdings by buying land, whether freehold or copyhold, and by leasing, enclosing and engrossing got together moderate-sized farms. They were the first men to farm on anything beyond subsistence level, the real creators of England's wealth and the backbone of its society.

The status of the yeoman could never be clearly defined by what he possessed. In the midlands many a yeoman was better off in lands and personal effects than the average northerner who signed *Gent* after his name, but poorer than many a Kentish husbandman who was considered a grade below him in rank, while the yeoman of Kent was rich compared with any other in the country:

> *A Knight of Wales,*
> *A gentleman of Cales,*
> *A Laird of the North Countree–*
> *A Yeoman of Kent*
> *Sitting on his penny rent*
> *Can buy them out all three.*

One can best define a yeoman not by comparing one with another but by considering his function within his own society. He was to the parish what the gentleman was to the county. He filled the ancient office of Churchwarden and as such was in Elizabethan times, apart from the parson, the chief parish officer and supervisor of its morals. At this time when the manor was decaying and the parish becoming the unit of local government, he was a member of the Vestry which met monthly to manage its affairs. He was obliged to serve when elected in the unpaid office of Overseer of the Poor, Bridge Warden, Surveyor of the Highways or parish Constable. Besides farming the land, many a yeoman carried on another trade such as pottery, saddlery, tanning, glass-making or carpentry.

The yeomen of England lived in sturdy houses of any size between cottage and large farmhouse, built of local materials, the cob of Devon, the granite of Cornwall, the yellow and grey stone of the Cotswolds, the drab limestone of the north-ern hills, the half-timber of the south-east and the black-and-white of Cheshire and the adjacent counties. They were men of worth if not always of great substance, and their wives, who, according to Fuller, "set up sail according to the keel of their husbands' estates", enjoyed a corresponding dignity and a standing such as few womenfolk had up to that time held. There was no room for idleness in a goodwife's life, for the management of the household was her vocation, the back-ground of a full and useful existence. "Goody" was mistress of her own establishment, skilled in every art and craft of housekeeping, the making of clothes, the brewing of beer, the lore of herbs and simple medicine, and the running of a house-hold which comprised not only her family but all the labourers and servants who worked for the Goodman. Like an efficient managing director, the wife of a well-to-do yeoman organis-ed the work of the household while the menial tasks were carried out by the wives and daughters of the labouring classes.

But again, one must speak generally, for there was no hard and fast rule in English society as to who was who. It is enough to say that of all the social grades, noble, gentleman, yeoman husbandman and labourer, the middle one was for two centuries and more the mainstay of the English social life. Its members not only provided England with its bread: from their ranks came some of the country's most distinguished lawyers, churchmen, doctors, scientists and writers. The "butcher of Norwich", father of Cardinal Wolsey, was a yeoman grazier. Harrison defines the yeoman as one who owned freehold land worth at least forty shillings a year, but even that qualification was not really necessary. Bishop Hugh Latimer said that his father, a Leicestershire yeoman, rented a farm "of three or four pounds a year at the uttermost, and hereupon he tilled so much as kept half-a-dozen men. He had walk for a hundred sheep and my mother milked thirty kine. He was able and did find the King a harness, with himself and his horse." On this rather meagre living Latimer's father sent his fourteen year old son to Cambridge. He was one of many.

The sixteenth and seventeenth centuries saw many elaborations and improvements in the building of the yeoman's medium-sized house. In southern and central England at least, thatch was still the most common way of covering a

Varieties of roof incorporating hip and gable

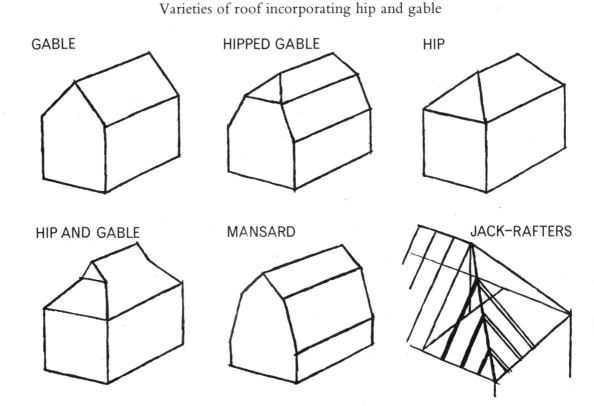

roof, but the ridge of a gabled roof was always a weak point, so to shorten this ridge many builders resorted to making hipped roofs. These were built on the same simple plan as the charcoal burner's structure mentioned on page 17, the thicker beam sloping down from the end of the ridge to the place where the wall-plates met at the angle of the roof. On these, rafters called jackrafters were laid, and they increased in length from the corner to the end of the ridge. Later it was found possible to construct many variants, the two chief of which were the hipped gable and the hipped roof with gables, terms which explain themselves.

By this time much more use was being made of bricks. For some unknown reason their manufacture in England ceased after the Romans left and no more were made until the twelfth century. They were first used principally for churches though one of the oldest known buildings in which brick was featured is Little Wenham Hall in Suffolk, a fortified manor house built round about 1275. By the early sixteenth century brick was the most fashionable of all materials for building, whether of churches or of mansions. It was more expensive than timber or plaster but was much cheaper than stone which had to be quarried and transported, sometimes over long distances. This was partly because bricks were generally produced locally. Also, all the bricks used for one building could be made uniform in size and shape, though in the fifteenth century sizes varied in different places. The general thickness was 2 in., the length between 9 and 11 in. Tudor and Stuart bricks are thicker, up to $8\frac{1}{2}$ in. by 4 in. by $2\frac{5}{8}$ in.

Owing to irregularities in baking, many early bricks became distorted in shape, and others were burnt a deep purple. These are often seen in the patterned walls and towers of some of our Tudor churches. The traditional way of laying them was in English bond, that is, alternate headers and stretchers with the second brick from the end of each line of headers (called a *closer*) laid on its narrow side to avoid vertical joints falling one immediately over another. The earliest work, when brickmaking and bricklaying were in their infancy is, however, much more irregular. All these early bricks, in spite of imperfections, were hard and serviceable, very resistant to damp, to extremes of temperature and to smoke.

In the south and east of England in particular, brick was used on a really grand scale for walls, battlements, towers, windows and chimneys. Brickmaking in fancy shapes became a craze, as many famous Tudor chimney stacks testify. One only needs to glance at photographs of Tattershall Castle in Lincolnshire (1433-40), the North Bar at Beverley, Yorkshire (1409), Herstmonceux Castle, Sussex (1415-40), Faulkbourne Hall (1439) and the famous gatehouse of the unfinished mansion at Layer Marney (c. 1520) both in Essex, to see the extent and scope of building in brick. The construction of a great house needed such a large number of bricks that it was often found necessary to set up a brickworks close by the site.

A house completely built of brick was too expensive for any but the rich, for preparing clay and moulding the bricks, which all had to be done by hand, was a long business. The yeoman did, however, find it better to use brick for one part of the house, the chimney breast and the chimney stack. This item was well worth the expense, firstly because in the centre of the house it gave direct heat to two ground floor rooms and convected heat to the two rooms directly above them, and secondly because, being sturdy, the chimney served as a prop for the whole building, making it possible to economise when wood was scarce, by using only short beams. Moreover, even if the house was damaged by fire, the brick chimney usually stood a good chance of being again usable as the focus of a rebuilding. When in 1666 London was destroyed by fire and not a house was left standing in the desolate area, the brick chimneys still remained erect and were often the only landmarks by which the unfortunate owner was able to see where his house had been. For these reasons brick was used for chimneys both in town and country.

In some of the western and south-western counties where

stone was plentiful, it had already come into general use for the building even of smaller houses. The dissolution of the monasteries (1536-40) encouraged its use still further, for where the abbeys and priories were not turned into private residences as, for instance at Lacock, they were used as quarries. Stow tells us that in London, Sir Thomas Audley who acquired the Priory of Holy Trinity in Aldgate Ward offered the church to the parishioners of St. Katherine Cree to replace their old one. When his offer was turned down, he promised it as a gift to anyone who would come and take it, but nobody came. He therefore had it demolished at his own expense, and "the workmen with great labour beginning at the toppe, loosed stone from stone and threw them downe whereby most of them were broken, and few remained whole, and those were solde verie cheape, for all the Buildings then made aboute the Cittie were of Bricke and Timber. At that time any man in the Cittie might have a cart loade of hard stone for paving brought to his dore for 6d or 7d with the carriage."

The same fate awaited hundreds of religious houses in England, especially in the eastern counties where stone was scarce. In Essex, for instance, which before the Dissolution had 44 of these houses, not one remains whole, and most have vanished altogether. In the same period many Roman remains were destroyed and carried off piecemeal by stone robbers. Among these were Silchester. This Roman provincial capital, which King John had seen as a pile of ruins, was levelled to the ground, its stone taken away and the plough driven over its site.

In the stone belt which extends from Dorset in the south-east to Lincolnshire and East Yorkshire, stone came into use in the sixteenth and seventeenth centuries for farm houses and even for cottages. It was ideal for the person who did not wish to build on a large scale, and it furnished the sturdy and cosy homes which still surprise us as we round the curves of many a country road. Outside the stone-bearing areas it was used sparingly. In the north, which was fully a hundred years behind the south-east in house construction and furnishing, stone was the natural building material but life in the lonely cottages on the bleak Pennines was and in places is today, simple and even rough.

In the more populous south, all the improvements Harrison writes about were to be seen in country towns and villages. Plaster was becoming popular everywhere. On the exteriors of half-timbered houses in the empty spaces between the studs and over the door the plaster was decorated with designs, usually simple geometrical shapes, either drawn on it with a comb when the plaster was wet, incised by series of points or raised in relief. This, called pargeting (probably from the French *parjeter*–throwing on), became most widespread during the seventeenth century when beams and studs, so prized by the antiquarian of today, were entirely overlaid with plaster to make more room for the decoration. As the seventeenth century progressed, true pargeting, with complicated designs and even reliefs of simple objects such as flowers, crowns and heraldic beasts was applied to external plastered walls, sometimes by using moulds, sometimes by modelling on a skeleton or outline of pins. Pargeting declined with the passing of the half-timbered house, but, like many old arts such as thatching, has been revived in the twentieth century. Meanwhile inside the house, lath and plaster came to be used to fill in the spaces between ceiling joists and finally to make the complete plain underdrawing, by covering the ceiling timbers altogether.

In olden days the household fire meant much more than it does today, for it was the only means of domestic heating and cooking, and in the humblest dwellings during the dark evenings there was rarely any other kind of artificial lighting. The axial chimney-stack (i.e. placed at the axis of the house between two inner walls) was, figuratively and literally, the prop of the house. In the smaller husbandmen's dwellings the old hood and flue was still in vogue, but more and more yeomen's living rooms had the wide chimneys and open fireplaces for burning logs, equipped with spits on racks above the great oaken lintel, iron pots and all the paraphernalia for cooking, while alongside was the ample inglenook large enough to take a chair. When the fire was out, one could peer up the chimney and see the sky above, and when the soot began to fall thrust holly branches up the wide funnel and clean the sides. Separate kitchens and parlours often had their own smaller chimney-stacks rising needle-like from the ends of the buildings.

In houses where the main chimney-stack was not axial, it was generally built as a projection on the outside of the building, a fashion which has lasted into the twentieth century, in spite of the loss of heat entailed. Its chief virtue was that the main construction did not have to be interfered with.

Ovens of brick and clay were built into the hearths, and often were to be seen from the outside, as round or rectangular projections standing out from the walls of the house. When the fire was raked out, the oven was hot enough for the baking of bread or the making of oatcakes on a bakestone or "backstone". One of the less important uses of the oven after baking was to keep warm a flat stone or oven plate which, well

Cotswold stone and stone slates. Cottages at Snowhill, Gloucestershire, with bread oven projecting from wall

wrapped up in cloth, served as a foot-warmer in bed. The better-off farmers who had separate kitchens could often afford detached bakehouses as well as cheese-chambers, apple-chambers and cornlofts. In the smaller houses the sides of bacon and cheeses were hung from the beams of the living-room and even the bedchambers, while the sacks of corn were stored in any suitable corner and apples and pears were laid in rows to keep through the winter, lying, as the poet John Drinkwater saw them

> *under the gloomy beams;*
> *On the sagging floor; they gather the silver streams*
> *Out of the moon, those moonlit apples of dreams,*
> *And quiet is the steep stair under.*

while the maturing harvest of field, garden and orchard mingled their pleasant homely odours and spread them through the whole house.

In most houses which were larger than the labourer's cottage the upper floor covered the whole ground floor and was an integral part of the house. The old loft-ladder at the far end of the living-room had also been supplanted by the fixed stair-case. This was either open, running alongside the living-room wall, or cased. Where there was an axial chimney-stack a con-venient corner for the staircase was found between the stack and an exterior wall, but in that case the stairs had to curve or turn at an angle. The medieval newel, though sometimes installed, was hardly suitable for the smaller house, and the carpenter often resorted to the dog's-leg design, making a complete turn halfway up the stairs, or, if there was more room, the open well staircase with two right-angle turns.

Earthen floors were still common, though in places where stone was plentiful, flags or slates were cleaner. Elsewhere cobbles and clay came in useful. Mixed with ox-blood and fine ashes, then pounded and levelled, clay became hard enough to bear the roughest treatment and could even be polished. Though most upper floors were of thick bare planks,

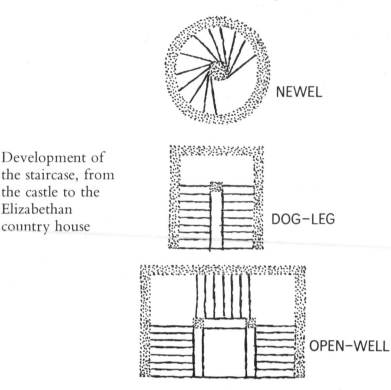

NEWEL

Development of
the staircase, from
the castle to the
Elizabethan
country house

DOG-LEG

OPEN-WELL

some were overlaid with plaster after the joists had been
packed with clay, but this had a tendency to crack as the wood
below shrank or warped.

It was the custom in England to spread hay, straw or rushes
on a floor. A visitor in 1578 saw the floor of Queen Elizabeth's
presence chamber at Greenwich strewn with hay. This made
cleaning easy, as it prevented dirt being trodden into the floor,
provided that the covering was changed often enough. If not,
the continuous tramping caused it to cake and harbour vermin.
Erasmus, who was in England between 1509 and 1513, evidently saw many dirty floors if we are to judge from a letter
he wrote to a friend: "The floors are commonly of clay,
strewed with rushes, under which lies unmolested an ancient
collection of beer, grease, fragments, bones, spittle, excrement
of dogs and cats and everything that is nasty."

By the end of the century, with the improvement of housing

and living standards, there was also probably an improvement in cleanliness, though the flea was still a common inhabitant of many homes. Thomas Tusser in his *Hundreth Good Points of Husbandrie* recommended the strewing of floors with wormwood.

> *While wormwood hath seed, get a bundle or twain,*
> *To save against March, to make flea to refrain.*
> *Where chamber is swept and that wormwood is strown,*
> *No flea for his life dare abide to be known.*

Ever since the days of the Romans, glass has been used in England, but it was very precious in the Middle Ages and mostly found in churches. In Tudor times glass became more plentiful and therefore cheaper, and men of substance cast away their wicker framework, their panels of horn and framed blinds of oil-soaked cloth called "fenestrals" and the craze for glass spread. The jingle about Hardwick Hall–"more glass than wall", a testimony to the wonderful new era of peace and expansion, could be repeated in connection with many other fine new houses. Glass was a boon even to the smaller man, letting in the light and keeping out the wind. Windows were fixed in moveable casements which could easily be taken out, and until 1579 their owners were accustomed to leave them in their wills, not with the estate but to their personal representatives. In that year, however, by a legal decision, glass fixed by nails to windows was no longer to be taken out "for without glass is no perfect house".

One sixteenth-century writer was very proud of his windows: "——Window leuys (leaves) of tymbre be made of bourdes joyned to gether with keys of tree let into them . . . I have many pretty windows, shette with leuys going up and down." This seems to imply that his windows could be opened and shut by means of some sort of sash. "Now," says William Harrison, "our lattices are also grown into less use because glass is come to be so plentiful and within a very little so good cheap, if not better than any other."

The old custom of hanging walls with tapestry persisted in the better-class houses well into the seventeenth century, for in creating air space between wall and room or covering a door these contributed greatly to the warmth indoors. In smaller houses painted cloth was used and great quantities imported from abroad. But as the draught-proofing of rooms through better-fitting doors and the insertion of window-glass proceeded, there was less and less need for it except as pure decoration or for door and window curtains. From time immemorial church walls had been adorned with wall paintings. Round about the thirteenth century the practice of painting walls spread into domestic use and by the sixteenth century it was fairly common in yeomen's houses. When the interior of smaller houses came to be plastered, the application of colour made them brighter, and here the yellow ochre, archil and copperas again found a use. Stone floors especially around the walls and fireplaces were made neat by the application of rubbing-stones or pipeclay and the rest of the floor strewn with yellow sand to make it easier to sweep. Even in this century an essential part of the Yorkshire and Lancashire housewife's stock-in-trade was the bright yellow scouring stone for the hearth and doorstep and the white one for outlining. Coloured walls were often decorated with designs stencilled on them in a darker shade.

Meanwhile the wealthier classes had taken to the putting up of wainscot, which was but another and more expensive method of beautifying a room and keeping in the warmth. The simplest form was the square or rectangular panel fixed between posts and rails, and the vertical arrangement of oaken boards tongued at one edge and grooved at the other. More elaborate patterns were the alternate double-tongued and double-grooved boards, and finally the much-treasured elaboration of this pattern known as linenfold.

In Elizabethan days another design appeared – the small panels, each with its own carving – an animal or bird or plant, a human face or an intricate design of flowing lines or leaf-shapes and, over the heavy oaken fireplace, a family heraldic device picked out in gold, silver and other brilliant tinctures.

One of the main uses of tapestry was on the bed. Harrison remarks on the elaboration of bed furnishings that took place even during his own lifetime:

"... our fathers, yea and we ourselves also, have lain full oft on straw pallets, on rough mats covered only with a sheet, under coverlets made of dagswain or hopharlots (I use their own terms), and a good round log under our heads instead of a bolster or pillow. If it were so that our fathers or the goodman of the house had within seven years after his marriage purchased a mattress or flock bed, and thereto a sack of chaff to rest his head upon, he thought himself to be as well lodged as the lord of the town, that peradventure seldom lay in a bed of down or whole feathers, so well were they contented, and with such base kind of furniture; which also is not very much amended as yet in some parts of Bedfordshire, and elsewhere, further off from our southern parts. Pillows (said they) were thought meet only for women in childbed. As for servants, if they had any sheet above them, it was well, for seldom had they any under their bodies to keep them from the pricking straws that ran oft through the canvas of the pallet and rased their hardened hides."

The advice of English physician Andrew Boorde, in his *Compendious Regiment or Dietary of Helth* (1542), was that a man should go to bed merry after having had pleasant company, "so that no anger nor heaviness, sorrow nor pensivefulness do trouble and disquiet you". He recommended a scarlet nightcap, a good thick quilt of cotton or of pure flocks of clean wool covered with white fustian, "and lay it on the featherbed that you do lie on, and on your bed lie not too hot nor too cold, but in temperance."

The featherbed was almost certainly a four-poster, the kind of bed in which Queen Elizabeth slept when she went on her progresses through the country in the three autumn months of almost every year. The first four-posters were strictly utilitarian, against draughts and, when many slept in one room, to ensure privacy. In Elizabethan days the bed with its carved pillars, tester, curtains and valances was one of the most valuable articles in the house. The bedroom itself might be furnished with no more than a chest and a stool, but the bed itself was a measure either of the owner's family pride or his present prosperity.

There was little indoor sanitation. The medieval castle keep had had its garderobes in the corner-towers on the second and third floors, with stone or wooden seats and chutes emptying into a moat or ditch, and these were copied in the larger houses, though not, for obvious reasons in timber-framed buildings. An improvement on the garderobe was the close stool of the Elizabethan gentlemen, but the peasant and even the yeoman could have had little more than a hole in the ground or a primitive cesspit probably covered by a wooden shelter and situated well away from the house. This was the forerunner of the outside lavatory of the nineteenth-century dwelling-house. For washing the hands, which was usual after meals since the fingers were still used for eating, the larger houses had ewers and hanging jugs, and almost every house by the end of the sixteenth century had its stone sink with outlet into the drain or soakaway outside. This was indeed a great luxury. Piped water was non-existent except in London and here only a few very privileged people were allowed "quills" to run it into their houses from the common water supply. Even Lord Burghley, Lord High Treasurer of England was refused permission to lead a pipe to his house and the Countess of Essex had her private supply cut off because her servants were using the water too lavishly.

The contrast between the housing of the rich and poor was more pronounced in the towns, since social classes had to live in such close proximity to one another, the rich in houses enclosed within their own grounds, the shopkeepers and craftsmen in their half-timbered dwellings standing in picturesque irregularity along the main thoroughfares, the poor closely packed together in tenements, hovels and cellars tucked away behind main streets. In the Middle Ages, as long as the towns did not expand too rapidly, the balance between the various classes was maintained, but in the sixteenth century developments took place which upset it.

These arose largely from the great rise in the number of unemployed throughout the country, and the drying up of the sources of charity with the dissolution of the abbeys and priories. Homeless and workless people took to the roads, which indeed was the only thing they could do when evicted, and England was faced with a problem which had never before arisen, that of the multitude of vagabonds, footpads and sturdy beggars thronging the highways. Ever since Roman times the town had offered to the destitute the doubtful prospect either of a job or of some way, honest or dishonest, of becoming rich. Tenements already overcrowded, became more so as landlords, seeking to benefit from the demand, added more storeys to their already overloaded properties, or extended them by digging cellars and putting up shacks in gardens and on every available plot of land.

The problem was naturally most acute in London, magnet of all poor fortune-hunters and suffering during the later sixteenth century from a veritable invasion of poor and destitute people. Stow tells us how they were housed. Land released through the Dissolution of the twenty-three religious houses was put on the market and built on. The grounds of St. Katharine's-by-the-Tower were enclosed and "pestered with small tenements and homely cottages having inhabitants English and strangers, more in number than in some cities in England". Noblemen who had possessed town houses within the gates were being driven by the "horrid fumes" from the increasing number of coal fires to migrate westwards into the prevailing wind, and to build new mansions on the bank of the river towards Westminster. They, too, sold their houses to speculators and many of these houses became tenements.

Northumberland House, the old home of the Percy family, was first turned into bowling alleys, then when these proved a nuisance they were destroyed by the Mayor and Sheriffs and the land used for building "a number of great rents, small cottages for strangers and others". The same thing happened to the Earl of Oxford's house in Lime Street. This house, being "greatly ruinated of late time, for the most part hath been letten out to Powlters for stabling of horses and storage of Powltrie, but now lately new builded into a number of small tenements letten out to strangers, and other meane people". Churchwardens, too, realising that money was to be made through letting property, built on their graveyards. St. Michael's Cornhill, realising that much of their valuable plate, vestments and ornaments would be confiscated to the state if they did not get rid of it, sold it between 1548 and 1551, realising £455, with which they built a number of tenements "whereby the Church is darkened and in other wayes annoyed". In spite of repeated proclamations from the year 1580 onwards, the building went on, and both inside and outside the walls as far as Mile End, St. Giles's and Westminster the blight of alleys and tenements spread, straining the water supply, overloading the drainage and spreading infection. What happened in London at that time also happened on a smaller scale in other cities of England.

We know from accounts and from parish records something of the state of the streets—the common field between Aldgate and Whitechapel crowded with filthy cottages, the slums of Westminster with their stinking alleys at the very gates of the royal palace, brimming with filth and inhabited by every kind of rogue and sharper. The Act of 1588, known as the Four Acre Act, which made it an offence to erect a cottage anywhere in England within a mile of the sea, except for workmen's or quarrymen's cottages, or unless there were four acres of land attached to it, was an attempt to stop overcrowding and to ensure that the occupants of new cottages should have enough land to provide them with a living.

Among its provisions were penalties for keeping lodgers. Though in all parts of the country the Quarter Sessions records give cases of persons apprehended for the infringement of this Act, it cannot have been strictly applied, or rather, its evasion was allowed often to go unnoticed, for the number of cottages and the multiplication of inmates in tenements went on growing. A letter from the Privy Council to the Justices of Middlesex ten years after the passing of the Act gives an idea of the kind of thing that went on in spite of acts and ordinances:

"You have had so many and spetiall directions from us . . to have spetiall care that no newe tenements should be erected in the suburbs of the Cytty, and notwithstandinge in divers places at this instant yt ys to be seene that there are many tenements and buildings now in hand, her Majestie fyndinge thereby juste occasion to conceave great offence both against you that by so many and often warnyngs have been charged to look to these continual abuses . . . Wee must let you understand your slacke and negligent oversight therein dothe deserve some sharp and severe reprehension . . . . . . We have thought good to warn you of your duties, to have better regarde hereafter to see this dysorder better looked into . . . . . . and especially at this tyme of the year . . . . *those that doe make newe buildings doe cause the frame to be made in other places and suddenly sett up the same.* Therefore you shall staie those buildings that are in hand, and binde the parties that doe cause them to be erected to answere the erectinge of them contrary to our orders. . . ."[1]

Reproofs and prohibitions did not have the slightest effect. They were avoided by stealth, bribery and other means and in the end the Crown nullified its own acts by giving licences to build in return for money. Thus the rich man built under licence, and the speculator without. The result was that while

[1] *The Growth of Stuart London,* by N. G. Brett-James (Allen and Unwin, 1935).

Narrow streets and tall, overhanging storeys. Sixteenth-century houses of wood and plaster at the corner of Chancery Lane and Fleet Street, London; taken down in 1791

the houses of the rich became more splendid, those of the poor were more jerrybuilt than ever and quickly deteriorated into the most hideous slums.

The state of the narrow alleys and back streets of the Elizabethan town is known, but we may not pass through the door of the damp, unventilated tenement room, the dark overcrowded cellar-dwelling or the hastily erected shack. The rest must be left to the imagination.

VI

The English Cottage

Mine be a cot beside the hill;
  The beehive's hum shall soothe my ear;
A willowy brook that turns the mill,
  With many a fall shall linger near.

The swallow, oft, beneath my thatch
  Shall twitter from her claybuilt nest;
Oft shall the pilgrim lift the latch,
  And share my meal, a welcome guest.

Before my ivied porch shall spring
  Each fragrant flow'r that drinks the dew;
And Lucy, at her wheel, shall sing
  In russet gown and apron blue.

The village church among the trees,
  Where first our marriage-vows were given,
With merry peals shall swell the breeze
  And point with taper spire to Heaven.

In these words Samuel Rogers, the banker-poet (1763–1855) drew his idyllic picture of the simple country life. The reality was very different from this.

In 1688 Gregory King estimated that there were in England 1,300,000 cottagers and paupers, and 1,275,000 "labouring people and outservants" with their families who were on much the same social level. Thus out of a total of $5\frac{1}{2}$ million, the "labouring poor", plus paupers but excluding vagrants, numbered approximately 2,575,000–nearly half the population.

What do we associate with the word "cottage"? What comes to mind first is "country". In spite of the rush to the towns in the sixteenth and early seventeenth centuries,

England was composed of countrymen. The absorption of the great floating population of vagabonds as a result of Elizabethan legislation and social adjustment had brought about a state of affairs in which whoever was found wandering without means of subsistence was whipped by the parish authorities and sent home. This enforced settlement brought about the erection of numerous small country dwellings inhabited not by the unemployed, but by the under-employed. The natural consequence was poverty. King classes the cottagers with the paupers, so easily did one merge into the other. The average family income of the cottager he estimates at £6 10s. per annum. To maintain this standard they had to work, but their work was seasonal and often casual. Many were day-labourers, dependent on others for their employment and living on wages fixed by the Justices of the Peace for their county. While working, the labourer had his food at his employer's table, but his wife and children were less fortunate.

Almost from the day he was able to walk, the labourer's child was made to bring pennies in by bird-scaring, running errands and stone picking. If children lived to be nine years old, for the death rate among the young of the labouring classes was high, they would probably go into service until marriage, when the drab life of the cottager or labourer was repeated in another generation. Their land was not their own, they were conditioned from their earliest days to submit to their betters and to pull the forelock, and only a minority of England's squires were as considerate to their dependants as Sir Roger de Coverley.

The housing of the poor was deplorable. C. E. Innocent (*The Development of English Building Construction*, 1916) states that the dwellings of the English agricultural labourers, not only at this period but long afterwards, were neither timber-framed nor of stone or brick, but hastily thrown-up constructions of branches, rushes and turf, of palings and hurdles, of wattle, clay and mud. If such was the case, how much worse off must have been King's "cottagers and paupers".

Joseph Hall (1574-1656), Bishop of Norwich and satirist, who saw and commented on the wretchedness of these poor dwellings believed that the standard of housing for the poor in his day was little better than it had been in Chaucer's time. His description might well be the same interior as that of Chaucer's poor widow:

> "Of one bay's breadth, God wot! a silly cote,
> Whose thatchèd sparres are furr'd with sluttish soote
> A whole inch thick, shining, like black-moor's brows,
> Through smok that down the head-les barrel blows:
> At his bed's feete feeden his stalled teme;
> His swine beneath, his pullen o'er the beame:
> A starved tenement, such as, I gesse
> Stands straggling in the wasts of Holdernesse:
> Or such as shiver on a Peake-hill side,
> When March's lungs beate on their turfe-clad hide."

Such a picture strips all the glamour from cottage life.

Besides the cottagers there were many others who might be classed as cottage-dwellers. Among the higher groups in King's classification come the freeholders, farmers, artisans and tradesmen with their families, numbering in all nearly two millions. Of these a very large proportion dwelt in moderate-sized houses which we today would call cottages. Unlike the frail hovel of the peasant, they were built to last and to give a measure of comfort. According to Gregory King, the cost of a labourer's house was approximately three times his yearly income, in all, about £45, which would in those days pay for the erection of a good sound building.

The latter part of the sixteenth century was a period of great economic advance, for the world was changing rapidly, and England with it. The discovery of distant lands increased the rewards that were to be gained from foreign trade, and the new chartered companies brought goods from the Levant, Russia, India, the Far East and the New World. The inflow of capital coincided with the need to produce goods both for home and export, and England passed through a minor industrial revolution as new industries were set up and old ones expanded. The promise of reward and the absence of restrictions gave every encouragement for the inventive and the adventurous. Internal peace and freedom from invasion made possible the building up of resources, and the social upheaval of the early century liberated a vast reservoir of labour. In its closing years England entered on an era of great material prosperity which affected all but the very lowest levels of society. The quantity of coal mined increased tenfold, the number of merchant ships fivefold, glass was manufactured in Sussex and the London soap boilers supplied all England. The production of Wealden iron and lead from the Mendips increased, the discovery of zinc ore made brass-founding possible and prospectors searched Cumberland for copper deposits. The domestic workers of Birmingham found markets for the nails, screws, hinges and locks they produced, and the first articles of cutlery began to appear from the small forges in the hills around Sheffield. Immigrants from the troubled Netherlands brought a new lease of life to the cloth trade of Essex and Suffolk. The revival of industry and agriculture meant a re-absorption of labour, a general rise in the standard of living and an increase in the demand for other products such as hemp, flax, leather, teazles, dyes, salt, fuller's earth and bricks. A higher standard of living meant greater demands on the part of the workers, and one aspect of this was the general desire for better housing. The hovel still remained, even into the nineteenth century, but the smallholder and the artisan who had risen out of penury asked for something better. The years 1550 to 1650 might well, therefore, be called the Century of the English Cottage.

In the Middle Ages the builders of castles and cathedrals could afford to have their materials brought long distances, even from foreign parts, but the village craftsman had no such advantage. He had to make the best use of what could be found in his own part of the country, and this depended on two things—geology and vegetation. In the south and east, where the forests grew most thickly, timber predominated; elsewhere whatever could be found was brought into service. Thus the cottage merges with the landscape of which it forms a part, the dark stone wall against the bleak Pennine hills, the granite cottage of the Cornish moor, the lichen-covered slates of the Cotswolds, the plaster, pargeting and thatch of the wheat counties. It is, as some writers have said, as if they have grown out of the ground on which they stand.

To a certain extent this is true. The country builder needed no architect to make elaborate plans. He knew what he wanted, and the end product was adapted in every way to the kind of life that he lived. There is an amazing diversity in the appearance of the cottages of England and in the materials from which they were constructed, but they have one thing in common. Whatever the need, in whatever part of the country, the cottage was made to fulfil it. It was the centre not only of family life, but also of industry, and as long as industry was carried on by hand, there was little need for change. A man built on the same lines as his ancestors had done, and many an eighteenth-century cottage could be mistaken for one of a much earlier date. He adapted and extended his dwelling as best pleased him, adding an outshut here or a second story with gabled window, embellishing his frontage with a carved oaken bressumer, breaking out the original plaster and substituting brick-nogging, or building a new chimney.

The beginning of the Century of the Cottage coincided with a general release of land, and the gentleman farmer was not the only person to benefit from it. In almost every manor there was a certain amount of waste, especially along the sides of the highways which, since they came under the control of the Justices of the Peace, had been made part of the responsibilities of the parish. Since the decay of the manor, it had been possible to dispose of manor lordships by sale, and the new lords, many of whom were merchants from the towns, regarded the manor as an investment from which to make a profit. Because the roadside waste was theirs to dispose of they began to convert it into small copyhold plots. For these the occupants paid annual quit-rents and on them erected small hutments with gardens, yards and workshops. As the property on the new copyholds increased in money value, so their value to the Lord of the Manor was increased, for every time one of them passed either by inheritance or by sale to another owner, he exacted a fine as manorial lords had always done, and this fine grew with the value of the tenement and the land it stood on. Thus a manorial lord who disposed of a hundred or more messuages in this way could draw from them a respectable and ever-increasing income. This enclosure of roadside waste was specially prevalent in the south-east, and old maps show many a wide roadway and village green which entirely disappeared between the seventeenth and nineteenth centuries. Where one-time villages have become small towns or residential areas, county councils are having to pay high prices to buy back land which was once common. In more isolated country districts, some of these tenements still stand and may be seen in twos and threes hugging the verge of a country road.

During this century the growing scarcity of timber brought about serious attempts to build in other materials. Brick had been used for great houses and churches since the fifteenth century. In the sixteenth it was adopted first sparingly for nogging and then extensively for houses and cottages. Tiles had long been used in London as a precaution against fire, and in the seventeenth century they came into more general use in other parts of the south-east. Where shrinkage had occurred between the timbers, a covering of tile was an easy and lasting remedy. Tile-hanging has always been a speciality of Kent, Sussex and Surrey. They were hung on battens either nailed into the oaken studs or, if they were on brick, as was sometimes the case, were nailed into the mortar. In most houses the tile-hanging was confined to the more exposed parts of the building such as the upper storeys and the gables. Where there

A good example of tile-hung cottages with overhanging upper storeys at Burwash, Sussex

Nicholas Wolmer's cottage, dated 1522, at Bletchingley, Surrey: a fine, tile-hung Tudor survival

was a better supply of local timbers, such as the Weald of Kent or Essex, much more use was made of weather-boarding. This is generally composed of long lengths of board laid with the lower edge of one over the upper edge of the one below. It became very popular in Essex during the nineteenth century, probably owing to its cheapness in comparison with other materials. While it cannot be described as beautiful, there is something pleasing in a weatherboarded cottage with the boards painted white, or even, as is seen near the coast, tarred a shiny black.

Ever since the Middle Ages the eastern counties of England have been open to influences from the continent. With the use of tiles came the mansard roof, an importation from France. Since the upper part had a low pitch and the lower part was near to the vertical, it offered more headroom in the upper storey into which were set dormer windows. From Holland came the pantile. Whereas the plain tile overlaps the two below it, that is, only one-third of it is covered, the pantile only overlaps one, but it also has a ridge on one side which overlaps an upturned ridge on the one next to it. These too were very popular from Suffolk to East Yorkshire. At first they were imported from Flanders and the earliest ones to be produced in England were at the factory at Tilbury in which Daniel Defoe was manager and chief owner.

From the seventeenth century onward, due partly to the need for more permanent buildings, partly to the growing scarcity of timber, there was a growing movement among cottage-builders towards the use of stone. East Anglia had none, apart from the north-west corner of Essex where a few cottages are built of it, and the district round Hunstanton, where walls and even houses are built of the beautiful and rather hard pinkish chalk found there. Norfolk also produces a coarse, gritty sandstone. Soft and light brown when quarried, it hardens and turns darker with exposure. Many cottage walls are built of it, sometimes alone, sometimes mingled with chalk. Apart from timber, these very imperfect materials, together with the clay lump built in large blocks were the only ones with which the people of East Anglia could build their homes.

The best stone-bearing country in England stretches in a wide belt from Dorset in a north-easterly direction across the Midlands and through Lincolnshire into north-east Yorkshire. The various kinds of limestone found in it are grouped by geologists under the name *oolite* (from the Greek *oion*—an egg) because the small granules of which they are composed resemble insect's eggs. Some parts of the belt contain better stone than others. One needs only to call to mind the names of some of the most famous quarries to trace out at least a part of it. Purbeck, associated with the marble so widely used in cathedrals and churches, also produces stone and slate. Some of the finest buildings in England are of stone from Bath and Portland. Corby, Ketton, Collyweston, Barnack and Stamford are only a few of the famous quarries in the east Midlands from which building materials have been drawn for centuries and transported all over the country. On one side of this belt, the north-west, lie the hilly regions of Wales and the Pennines with their scarcity of timber and their grey and more sombre sandstones and limestones, while on the other side, the south-east, is the predominantly timber region with the exception of the chalk and limestone of East Anglia and the quarries of Sussex and Kent. While much of the stone of these two regions is unsuitable for large and ornate buildings, all of it has been used in some way or other in the construction of the English cottage.

Starting just north of Bath and extending in a wide arc roughly parallel with the rivers Severn and Avon are the Cotswold Hills. Here, from medieval times, lived the shepherds and merchants on whom depended a large part of England's wool trade. Unencumbered by urban development, the pleasant valleys of the Cotswolds contain some of the finest old cottages in the country. The stone of which they are built is neither as good nor as uniform as the best Portland or Bath stone, but its rich colourings have made the Cotswolds one of England's show places which no serious traveller would miss seeing. Wherever in this area one wished to build there was a quarry very near, which could not only supply richly coloured stone for walls, but also serviceable limestone slates for roofing. Soft when taken from the quarry, Cotswold stone was easy to work, could be hewn into building blocks, even for the humble cottage, and could be used in places where normally wood or lead was needed. Thus we see windows in leaded panes, cased in wrought iron and set in mullions of stone. Sometimes both doors and windows are protected by carved drip mouldings. Wide-arched stone fireplaces may be seen inside the living-rooms, while outside are the projecting ovens with their semi-circular or rectangular slated roofs.

Cotswold stone slates were once to be seen almost everywhere, even on farm buildings, but with the coming of cheaper roofing materials they are now much more rare. When brought from the quarry the great slabs of slate were left exposed for a whole winter so that the frost could work on them and the ice penetrate and crack them open. The laying of a slate roof was a matter needing considerable skill, for the pieces were often of uneven and unequal thickness, and had to be carefully matched. Since they tended to curve slightly, it was necessary to pitch the roof at a steeper angle than normal, usually between 50 and 55 degrees. This in its turn created another characteristic of the Cotswold cottage, for the roof tended to come so low that there was no room under the eaves for the upper storey windows. These were therefore set in large gabled dormers, their ridges almost as high as the roof itself. Because of this the Cotswold roof had many "valleys" or joints between roof and roof or between roof and dormer. To cover these, the slaters used pieces of irregular shape and by fitting them skilfully, made "swept valleys" or graceful curves down which the water flowed as down a gutter, to find its way to the ground. Once laid, a roof of Cotswold slate was capable of lasting longer than the wooden battens supporting it, and the slight sag seen on some Cotswold cottages rather adds to than detracts from their appeal. Such villages as Broadway, Bourton-on-the-water, the Slaughters, and country towns such as Tetbury and Painswick occupy a place of their own in the English panorama.

The stone spine of England contains many cottages, but none so varied nor in such an attractive setting. The Romans quarried oolite in the Stamford district, and Barnack in the Middle Ages supplied stone for many a castle and abbey even as far south as Essex and the Thames estuary, to which it was taken by ferry. All Northamptonshire and Leicestershire are strewn with market towns, farms and cottages of true medieval type, with house-part and loft, and sometimes a parlour. As we approach Lincolnshire the mansard roof begins to appear. Dutch influence shows itself on the increase in the proportion of pantiles, and the characteristic stepped gable, an ornament commonly found only in eastern England. But apart from this the simpler and more homely dwellings are devoid of non-essentials.

As we move north and west of this line we come to the wilder scenery of the Derbyshire Peak and the Pennines, relieved by the Midland Gap of lower, richer land which reaches out towards the Cheshire Plain. Here once more, timber and plaster appear in unusual combinations, but in the north stone is the prevailing building material.

For variety in scenery the north of England is a world in itself. Lush valley, windswept moor, mountain and lake are all within reach of the half-day excursionist. Here a drop of a thousand feet in altitude within a distance of a mile or two can alter the temperature from spring to summer. Yet in the make-up of the smaller houses and cottages, there are many points of similarity. At a time when the lower lands were better forested the cruck dwelling appears to have been the main habitation of the household and farm unit, the lower part of the building often filled in with stone. Then, as wood became scarce and building techniques improved, stone became universal.

The rocks found in almost every part of the north are the coarser sandstones and limestones and the prevailing colour is grey. This does not make them any less suited to their purpose nor detract from their beauty, for grey is a colour which tones harmoniously with all natural tints. The magnesian limestones which stretch in a narrow strip from Nottingham to Ripon and thence extend in a widening triangle to the coast between Tees and Tyne have provided stone for innumerable churches in the north, as well as for York and Beverley Ministers and have been carried as far as the Thames valley where they form part of Westminster Hall, the Houses of Parliament and Greenwich Hospital.

Of the seven rivers which flow from the Pennines into the Yorkshire Ouse, three, the Aire, Calder and Don, pass through the coal-bearing rocks. Before the nineteenth centuries the West Riding, relying mainly on water power for its wool industry, had very little use for the coal which lay below it, but the rocks associated with the Coal Measures, the carboniferous sandstones, as they are called, were ideal for building the humbler cottages of the people. Here, even today, one might journey along a country road, or even in the outskirts of a manufacturing town and see huge artificial cliffs made by the quarrying of this stone. Their surfaces are gouged and broken as if great masses have been cracked off. In the newer quarries chunks of stone, sometimes of gigantic size, lie on the level sandstone floor where heaps of waste, soft yellowish scaly material, are piled up in corners for use on the roadways.

The older houses in these parts are built of this carboniferous sandstone, their walls made up of large blocks a foot thick and up to eighteen inches long, sometimes left rough, sometimes smoothed with well-fitting mortared joints. When new the best quality stone is light fawn in colour, but turns greyish with age. In these West Riding villages, one may see old cottages built of irregular courses of stone, here a large block twice the width of two narrower ones which continue the double course as far as the next large block, which may be one course lower down. The cottages are clustered together in

Single-storey 18th-century stone cottages a Bradford, Yorkshire. The small constructions in the fore ground were formerly used as privies a ashpits

Two-storey cottages near Bradford with irregular courses of sandstone, one re-roofed with Welsh slate and of the type formerly inhabited by weavers and woolcombers

"folds", "lumps" and yards, or in short rows of one- and two-storey dwellings, and older inhabitants still remember them by the names they bore before streets were officially named – Stocking (stockingers') Row, Collier Row, Spindle Row, Widow Row, Chapel Fold, Boot and Shoe Yard, Saddlers' Lump.

Home life in one of these is vividly described in the work of a northcountry antiquarian, William Scruton:

"The cottage in which we lived was situated in the very midst of a village near to Bradford, where the people were nearly all weavers and combers, and consisted of only two rooms; that is upstairs and down. The floors of these rooms consisted of rough heavy flagstones. On one side of the fireplace there was a large stone built into the wall which served for all sorts of things and uses. The back part was lined with large plates, and over them was a large wooden rack fastened to the wall which held the cups and saucers and smaller plates. Opposite, there stood under the window my mother's loom, and under the southern window my father's loom. At the west end of the room there stood a large shut-up bed. A three-legged table stood in the middle of the room, where we took our daily meals together. . . . Every evening the large pitcher was sent to the farmhouse for two quarts of milk. A large iron pot was set on the fire as we got up in the morning, which was between six and seven, both summer and winter. Water was put into the pot with a little salt, and a sprinkling of oatmeal on the top to keep in the steam. When it boiled, mother made porridge with oatmeal, and the weavers who were at work and all the rest had breakfast. At noon we had dinner of boiled potatoes and a bit of fried bacon, and if mother thought she could spare it, a small piece of bread each. . . . At one o'clock all into work again until evening, when we had porridge again, the same as in the morning, but with plenty of new milk. This was our diet all the year round, except that on Sunday afternoons we had tea in gill pots, and generally a currant cake each which mother had prepared for us. In the winter-time we had to light up with dirty, smoky, tin oil-lamps, which hung at the side of the loom, giving little light, and literally making darkness visible. I do not know any sight so gloomy as the weaving and combing rooms of those days when there was no gas as now. Still we were very happy, and the only dread was the lot of mills building and the steam looms displacing our employment."

This kind of scene, which must have been common about the year 1825, was drastically altered within ten years when the dreaded power-loom herded weavers into the new factories. Most of these old houses still stand, some in short blocks, others in irregular clumps as if thrown down haphazard. These clumps are today often connected by what was once a straggling village street made up of houses built with no perceptible building line and no uniformity. The 15–18 in. thick walls give "window bottoms" wide enough to carry an assortment of ornaments and house plants. The yards in front of the cottages are often paved with large oblong flagstones, and two extra big ones, one overlapping the other, are laid on the small rectagular block which is the outside privy, often situated by the front gate abutting on the street. Floors, too, are flagged, and the stone stairs leading to the first storey are worn down at the edges by generations of boots and shoes that have gone up and down them. The roofs are of sandstone slates, low-pitched, even as low as 35 to 25 degrees, because of their weight and thickness.

Long ago these cottages resounded with the hum of the spinning wheel and the clack of the handloom which stood by the window of the living room or in the upstairs working chamber, while in the cottages where wool was combed was the central post with nails from which fleeces were hung. Even today stone is everywhere.

The advent of power-driven machinery drowned the original small communities in a mass of modern and more regular streets of terrace houses. These are built of blocks of equal size in monotonous rows and their roofs of Welsh slate, sometimes holed with attic windows, tower high over their older and more tumble-down neighbours. In many places the old is joined to the new and it may be clearly seen where the one ends and the other begins. With steam power and the newer terrace house came the soot which has turned all, old and new, to a uniform blackness, black roofs and chimneys, black walls, gardens often a blaze of colour growing out of the blackest of black earth; only the stone flags of the pavements worn grey or light-brown through the passing of myriad feet.

We follow these tributaries of the Ouse up their valleys and track them to their sources. Now the stone becomes harder and more unmanageable. It breaks up into oddly-shaped irregular blocks and here dry stone-walling is much more of an art than in the lower reaches. Near to the borders of North Yorkshire and Lancashire, walls and houses are dark-grey, and the sheep that appear like dots on field and moor are hardly, as in Cornwall, distinguishable from stones. Millstone grit and carboniferous limestone with all their colours ranging from light-grey to brown are in keeping with the rugged and almost treeless landscape. Stone roofs and the stone walls of houses sometimes covered by a coat of whitewash go to make villages which were once, as in the days of Charlotte Brontë, "stone pillars where four roads meet" and no more. Here is wild rolling country whipped by every wind, with views extending for miles, and along the almost bare sweeping slopes, a long zig-zag line marking the limit up to which the land has been tamed, on this side a chequerwork of fields separated from each other by crooked tumbling limestone walls, on the other, open moorland, dark-green, brown or purple according to the season, and along this line the scattered farmsteads, squat, deep-gabled and low-roofed with stone slates. Their windows are small and encased in slabs larger than those making up the rest of the wall. Their barns, stables and storehouses are, for the sake of convenience, either part of the main building or standing off from it in numerous outshuts with the rectangular sloping roofs. This is the land of Windyridge and Wuthering Heights, each house standing lone near the moor's edge, its only link with the highway a narrow private cart-track. In contrast, other villages which but for the grimmer outlines of their houses might well be part of Devon or Dorset, set in pleasant gardens and orchards, nestle at the foot of the craggy hills.

In the long twilight of the English history when the Teutonic tribes took possession of the greater part of the country, the Britons whom they failed either to kill or absorb, fell back on the mountain fastnesses of Strathclyde (Cumberland and Westmoreland), Wales and Cornwall. Thus the oldest tribes came to occupy the lands where the oldest rocks, bared by ages of erosion, had come to the surface. Here the relentless struggle with nature for existence is typified in the cottages of granite, the walls of slate and the piles of rough stone which they made into homes. Devonshire achieved prosperity in the sixteenth century but it was not until the nineteenth that the lakeland was brought to the notice of the public by the poets, and hardly until the twentieth that tourism began to alter the face of Cornwall and Wales. Meanwhile in all parts of the country the cottages once inhabited by peasants and their families came to increase a hundredfold in value and were put on the market as desirable residences, renovated and fitted up with all modern conveniences, for the middle-class executive and wealthy business-man who sought temporary respite from the cares of the modern city.

For two centuries the English cottage performed a unique function. Economically it was necessary to the wellbeing of the community whose living depended on the exertions of the freeholder and the agricultural labourer. The first half of the eighteenth century, when towns were growing and absorbing the products of the countryside, was a time of growing prosperity. Foreign visitors to England were impressed by the good food, the neat clean cottages of the farmers and working people and the neat dress of their womenfolk. Cobbett looked back on the period as the golden age of rural England.

It was not to last. Ever since Tusser wrote his *Hundreth Good Points of Husbandrie*, there had been a growing interest in improving methods of agriculture. Jethro Tull (1674–1741) had invented a new seed drill and a method of hoeing land with horses; Lord Townshend (1674–1748) had improved yields by a new rotation of crops; Robert Bakewell (1725–1795) experimented in inter-breeding and produced improved breeds of both sheep and cattle. New grasses and root crops were introduced which made it possible to keep stock alive all winter instead of killing off large numbers in autumn. England was on the verge of a new era in agriculture, but this new era could not arrive without the investment of large amounts of capital in the land, and this meant the displacement of the small unit of cultivation, the strip in the open fields, by the large unit, the consolidated farm covering hundreds of acres. The capital was available; the land could only be got by enclosing the remaining commons and buying out the smaller men, the freeholders.

Every enclosure required an act of Parliament. Between 1700 and 1710 there was only one, but as the century passed the impetus towards enclosure grew. Between 1750 and 1760 there were 156 acts, between 1770 and 1780, 642, between 1800 and 1810, 906. In the previous period of enclosures during Tudor times less than one per cent of the total arable land had been affected and even that had brought about a social upheaval. The enclosures of 1750–1810 dispossessed thousands of families of their small plots of land. Many were reduced to the status of landless labourers, others migrated to the towns where they were absorbed into the growing number of workers in the new textile factories and the mines.

One of the chief results of this disruption of social life was the decay of the village. When the commons had gone the cottager lost his rights to gather wood and to pasture out his beasts; with the transference of industries to the towns the labourer's wife lost the domestic work with which she had supplemented the family income. With the rise in corn prices a man's wage, even if he worked full time, was not enough to

Timber and brick neighbours: two old cottages at Easling, Surrey

keep his family. The social historian tells us how towards the end of the century more and more labourers were compelled to seek relief from the overseers of their parishes and how the miserable wages of labourers, even those working full time, were, in certain parts of England, made up out of the parish poor rates. Their lot varied. Gilbert White, in his *Natural History of Selborne*, describes conditions in the Hampshire village of Oakhanger:

"We abound with poor; many of whom are sober and industrious, and live comfortably in good stone and brick cottages, which are glazed, and have chambers above stairs: mud buildings we have none. Besides the employment from husbandry, the men work in hop gardens, of which we have many, and fell bark and timber. In the spring and summer the women weed the corn. . . . The inhabitants enjoy a good share of longevity: and the parish swarms with children."

No less pleasant is Crabbe's description, in *The Village*, of a country cottage in the early nineteenth century

> *Behold the Cot! where thrives th'industrious swain,*
> *Source of his pride, his pleasure and his gain;*
> *Screened from the winter's wind, the sun's last ray*
> *Smiles on the window, and prolongs the day;*
> *Projecting thatch the woodbine's branches stop,*
> *And turn their blossoms to the casement's top:*
> *All need requires is in that Cot contain'd,*
> *And much that taste untaught and unrestrain'd*
> *Surveys, delighted. . . . . .*

The worst side of cottage life, and probably the most prevalent if we are to go by parish records of the time, is to be seen when he leaves the "fair scenes of peace", and "vice and misery demand the song".

> *We turn our view from dwellings neat*
> *To this infected row we term our street. . . . .*
> *Between the roadway and the walls offence*

Invades all eyes and strikes on ev'ry sense:
There lie, obscene, at every open door
Heaps from the hearth and sweepings from the floor,
There hungry dogs from hungry children steal,
There pigs and chickens quarrel for a meal;
There dropsied infants wail without redress,
And all is want, and woe and wretchedness.

To every house belongs a space of ground,
Of equal size, once fenced with paling round;
That paling now by slothful waste destroy'd,
Dead gorse and stump of elder fill the void;
Here is no pavement, no inviting shop,
To give us shelter when compelled to stop;
But plashy puddles stand along the way
Filled by the rain of one tempestuous day,
And these so closely to the buildings run
That you must ford them for you cannot shun;
Though here and there convenient bricks are laid,
And doorside heaps afford their dubious aid.

Sheer misfortune or indolence? Goldsmith in a few lines (*The Deserted Village*) repeats the complaints voiced two hundred years before his time, during the first Tudor enclosure period:

The man of wealth and pride
Takes up a space that many poor supply'd:
Space for his lake, his park's extended bounds,
Space for his horses, equipage and hounds;
The robe that wraps his limbs in silken sloth,
Has robb'd the neighbouring fields of half their growth;
His seat, where solitary sports are seen,
Indignant spurns the cottage from the green.

Goldsmith wrote at the beginning of the great transformation. Cobbett (*Rural Rides*) at the end of it views the dilapidation into which the cottage had fallen:

" . . . . . go down into the villages, ... view the large,

and once the most beautiful, churches; see the parson's
house, large, and in the midst of pleasure-gardens; and
then look at the miserable sheds in which the labourers
reside! Look at these hovels, made of mud and of straw;
bits of glass, or of old cast-off windows, without frames or
hinges frequently, but merely stuck in the mud wall. Enter
them, and look at the bits of chairs or stools; the wretched
boards tacked together to serve for a table; the floor of
pebble, broken brick, or of the bare ground; look at the
thing called a bed; and survey the rags on the back of the
wretched inhabitants; and then wonder if you can that the
gaols and dungeons and treadmills increase. . . . ."

The Speenhamland system, where it was applied, of making
up the wages of the labourer out of the parish poor rate, had
taken from him every shred of self-respect. Misfortune had,
as it so often does, bred indolence. The Poor Law Commission's Report of 1834 gives numerous instances. Arthur
Young in 1801 put the point into the labourer's own mouth:

"Go to an alehouse kitchen of an old-enclosed country,
and there you will see the origin of poverty and high poor-
rates. For whom are they to be sober? For whom are they
to save? (Such are the questions). For the Parish? If I am
diligent, shall I have leave to build a cottage? If I am sober,
shall I have land for a cow? If I am frugal, shall I have half
an acre of potatoes? You offer no motives; you have nothing but a parish officer and a workhouse!–Bring me another pot."[1]

There is another side to the picture. Without the increased
production resulting from enclosures, England would never
have survived the twenty-two years of almost continuous
warfare with Napoleon. Even on the social side, the picture is
not entirely dark. In many a village the old cottages had been
crowded together round the main street and were grossly
overcrowded. Young in 1773 wrote, "Cottages are in general

[1] *England in Transition*, Mary Dorothy George
(Routledge & Kegan Paul Ltd., 1931).

the habitations of labourers, who all swarm with children, and many have double, treble, and even quadruple families." Though disaster faced the villages, the national conscience demanded that something be done for the labourer. Some landowners built for themselves new houses on their estates and the old ones were converted into habitations for the labourers. At the same time, since the commons disappeared, the miserable hovels that had been erected on them by squatters were no more. Many landlords took a pride in building decent cottages for their workpeople and the Board of Agriculture urged them to do all they could to improve the condition of their tenants' dwellings. As early as 1750 Lord Dorchester built a new model village, Newton Abbas, and this was followed by others at Lowther in Westmoreland, and at Harewood in the West Riding, on the estates of the Lascelles family, but these were built rather for the convenience of the owners than the satisfaction of the tenants.

In the early nineteenth century humanitarian motives inspired other wealthy men to undertake similar projects. Samuel Whitbread of Southhill built the village of Old Warden, and the row of semi-detached cottages on the estate of the Russell family at Ampthill, both in Bedfordshire, were among the earliest of the century. For the first time, the planning, siting and design of the cottage began to be the concern of the philanthropist as well as of the professional architect. Richard Elsam, writing in 1816 soon after the end of the Napoleonic War, gave the nineteenth-century version of Lloyd George's plea for "Homes for heroes to live in".

"Now the blessings of peace are restored to these happy isles by the united efforts of our countrymen, who have bled in the field of battle to protect our civil rights and independence, it is the happy moment when we should turn our eyes towards the condition of the poor, and . . . as monarchs, statesmen and philosophers of all ages have concurred in opinion, that the riches of a nation are the people, it is doubtless the duty of those in whose hands Providence has placed the means, to assist in promoting their welfare. The comforts and advantages derived in Society by their laborious exertions, make it absolutely necessary that the greatest pains should be taken to improve their condition. It is therefore a subject of deep concern that the miserable state of their habitations in many parts of these countries has never been seriously taken into consideration."

Elsam's contribution was the point put once again that to help the labouring poor by providing decent dwellings was more than charity; it was plain commonsense and in the national interest. Two years later the architect J. B. Papworth, inspired by similar motives, published his book *Rural Residences*, which included designs for cottages and workers' dwellings:

"The broken casement, the patched wall, the sunken roof, the withered shrub are corresponding testimonials of the husbandman's relaxed energies and broken spirit".

What the rural worker needed was nothing elaborate but a simple unostentatious cottage, for "the symbols of ease and luxury are at variance with the labourer's busy life and frugal means, and ought to be omitted." Nevertheless, the building should have grace and be well proportioned, displaying the elements of beauty generally associated with the simple life.

The ideas of the cottage reformers were taken up, but the model villages and isolated cottages put up in the early years of the nineteenth century were too few to touch the main problem of the agricultural workers. The remedy was to be delayed a hundred years, and was to be a political one when the problem of creating better cottages was to be merged into the greater one of working-class housing.

VII

The Building Revolution

Between the 2nd and 5th of September, 1666, the city of London, including a large area outside the walls as far west as the Temple, was destroyed by fire. This destruction would probably never have happened had the buildings not been almost entirely of wood and plaster. Other materials had been available for more than a century, but as often happens nature had to take a hand in the work of destruction before a new London could take shape.

In its structure, its architecture, its decoration and general appearance this new city was so utterly different from the old that anybody returning to it might well have imagined he was entering some mysterious new world. Gone was the ramshackle, ill-kept half timber with its sagging wall-plates, its lurching upper storeys, its jetties under which he was wont to take shelter, and the jutting shop-fronts thrusting themselves out into the roadway. Gone were the blacks and the whites, the dingy greys of neglected buildings, the dark interiors: instead long, straight rows of two- and three-storey houses, frontages of bricks glowing red and purple, plain square windows, iron railings and solid-looking doors with steps leading up to them. The only timber visible was built into the flat shop-fronts, and this was gaily painted, most unlike the grey and darkbrown oak he was used to.

A revolution in building had changed the face of London. Though new to the returning citizen, the change had nothing sudden about it. It was the result of a century of building development, packed into the limited space of two square miles.

There were two main elements in this building revolution.

The first was the use of brick. Rare in the fifteenth century, it had become very popular in the early sixteenth among the wealthy classes who experimented with all kinds of brick constructions including elaborate chimney-stacks, gables, ornamentation for porches, church furnishings, pulpits and even fonts. By the end of the Tudor period, brickmaking was a widespread local industry in the south and east, a region which, wherever suitable earth could be obtained, was dotted with brickfields. Once made, bricks were easier and swifter to handle than stone and had a multitude of uses even before they became the principal building material of the smaller house. Once their use was established the shape of the town house underwent changes.

Firstly, since the upper storey needed no wooden supports, the overhang tended to disappear, and the sag of the upper floor was obviated by placing joists on the narrow sides instead of, as had up to this time been the custom, on their wide sides. With bricks it was also possible to build upwards and in doing so increase the amount of headroom. Thus rooms came to be loftier, more airy and more spacious.

Towards the end of the Tudor period, coal, which had formerly been used only in industry, came into general domestic use. To distinguish it from the old "coal", now called charcoal, which was still being made in large quantities for gunpowder and iron-smelting, this domestic fuel was known as sea-coal because it was brought to London and the east coast towns by boat from the Northumberland coalfield. Coal being slower burning than wood or peat, it was possible to use smaller grates, to make chimney breasts much narrower and to restrict the width of chimney openings so much that a man could no longer climb up to clean them, and the chimney-sweeping for the next two and more centuries had to be done by boys. Both these innovations, the use of brick for building and coal for heating, gave far greater scope to the builder to experiment and to try out new ideas. This he had already done in the great houses with their imposing doorways, turrets, bays, expansive windows, galleries and staircases. In the smaller house the hall lost its importance as the general feature of the building, and eventually became little more than an entrance chamber. Thus, though we still call our great houses "So-and-so Hall", using the word in its old sense, the same word is used for what it eventually became in the modern terrace house, the poky little passage whose only feature is a doormat, a mirror and a few coat-hooks.

In the smaller house, the important room became the living-room, while in the larger house it was the reception or dining-room. But, with the coming of new materials and techniques, all the other rooms tended to become larger and more ornate. The disappearance of oak beams from walls and ceilings made it possible to cover them entirely with plaster. The walls were then often painted or, in more humble style, stencilled in regular patterns. Another way to ornament them was to cover them with painted or stencilled cloths stretched out on frames. Towards the end of the seventeenth century these painted cloths were replaced by plain canvas and on this was pasted large pieces of paper with pictures and designs painted on them. Later, the paper came to be pasted on the wall itself, but since it was hand-painted and therefore expensive, only the more wealthy could afford it. In 1712 a tax was put on paper for walls, and until this was repealed in 1860 it was not often to be seen in the humbler home. Wainscot continued to be used and, with a smaller fireplace, the possibilities of ornamentation with shelves, wainscot, coats of arms and other devices, were infinite. Meanwhile, the importance of the bedchamber continued to increase. In the Saxon hall there had been no privacy; in the castle the bedroom had been in the dark corner of a turret chamber. Now privacy was not a luxury but a necessity, and the bedroom had as much attention in decoration and furnishing as any other.

The rapid disappearance of the forests and the necessity to find other materials for building led to the gradual eclipse of the all-timber house. Fewer and fewer, even in the home

A Jacobean brick mansion continuing the Tudor tradition–
central tower, bays, turrets, ornamental gables and clustered
chimneys. Blickling Hall, Norfolk

counties were constructed during the seventeenth century.
The traditional plan of the old timber hall, however, remained
for some time. Many farmhouses in the provinces, though
some were built of stone and brick, still retained the cross-
passage from front to back, with two upper-chambered rooms
on the one side, that had once been the hall and parlour beyond
it, and another room on the opposite side of the passage, the
old buttery or pantry also with a chamber over it. Other
smaller country houses kept to the two-part plan, a hall with
chambers over it, and a wing, with a great chimney-stack
serving both.

Now, however, since there was more building than ever
before, more thought was also being given to the creation of
the most convenient house, and the services of the professional
planner, who had previously been employed only by the great,

came to be demanded by the more prosperous farmers. As a result, the Jacobean farmhouses, solid-looking rectangular buildings without wings, porches or any external embellishments, and with all the services compactly arranged under one roof, came into existence. These were functional, labour-saving and admirably suited to their purpose. The entrance door of the Jacobean farmhouse, instead of being placed to one side of the building, was in the middle, and the hall ran from front to back, with the staircase arranged in one part of it, containing usually either the well or dog-leg pattern of stair according to its size.

In some Jacobean houses the severe lines of the elevation were broken by the insertion of an arched window in the landing of the staircase. Though some of these houses were gabled, especially in the stone-bearing counties, the majority were either hipped or, in a few cases, had hipped gables. By the time this kind of house was being built, striking new ideas caused great changes in the appearance of domestic architecture both in town and country.

These arose from the visit of Inigo Jones, a young protégé of the Earl of Pembroke, to Italy where he went to study landscape painting. While there he transferred his interest to architecture and became an admirer of the style of the Italian architect Andrea Palladio (1518-80) who, in revolt against the extravagance of earlier architects, had revived the stately and formal style of the buildings of ancient Rome. Jones returned to England in 1605, and was introduced into the court of James I where he was employed principally to design the scenery for masques of which the King and Queen were very fond. Later he was made Surveyor-General of the Royal Buildings and as holder of this office became the most influential of all builders of his day. Of his own work, little except the banqueting House in Whitehall and the Queen's House in Greenwich still remains, but his importance lies in the ideas he brought from Europe and developed in England at a time when the country was at the height of its fortunes and so much building was going on. His ideas were readily adopted and he had many talented followers, among them his nephew, John Webb, and Sir Roger Pratt who expressed them in visible form in such buildings as Wilton House, Wiltshire, and Coleshill, Berkshire. These ideas, first applied to the large mansion, came to be adopted later for the humbler villa and farmhouse, and eventually even to the ordinary town house.

Jones's architecture was based on certain firm principles, some of them very un-English. The first was that before a stone was laid the whole conception must be thought out and put on paper. The men who planned the rebuilding of London after the Great Fire of 1666 carried this principle out to the letter by designing four standard types of house, from which no builder was to be allowed to depart, and also by specifying in detail where and in which street each type of house was to be built. In this respect alone Jones deserves to be regarded as the father of English architects.

Secondly, the building must be balanced. This was achieved by a large central block with wings symmetrical in most of their features. Thirdly, he stipulated that the building should be "masculine and unaffected". To achieve this he relied on clear lines, vertical and horizontal, columns rising up the facade, rectangular windows, and, following the Italian fashion, a basement. Above this, raised to about half a storey's height, was the "Floor of Honour", on which were the principal reception rooms and dining rooms. This floor was reached from the outside by a handsome flight of steps rising to a columned portico. Celia Fiennes, who travelled through England on horseback just before 1700, described it as she saw it at Coleshill:

> "The house is new built of stone, most of the offices are partly under ground–kitchen, Pantry, buttlery and good Cellers and round a Court is all the other offices & out houses; The entrance of the house is an ascent of severall steps into a hall so lofty the roof is three storyes, reaches to the floore of the gallery. . . ."

"The building must be balanced." Burgh House, Hampstead:
an example of the principles enumerated by Inigo Jones

So many of these features became at one time or another part of the domestic architecture in England that one might even now pick them out by looking at pictures of houses by Jones or his pupils and comparing these with others of different periods, even with the terrace house that one finds in London and the provinces, and noting the points of similarity. His ideas were modified by Wren and the London architects of the 'sixties.

Take in the first place, the post-Fire houses of London. When the city was to be rebuilt, Charles II appointed six commissioners to submit to him and to the Privy Council plans for the new houses and streets. Of these, two, Roger Pratt and Hugh May, were followers of Inigo Jones, and both were men of wide experience and great ability. The third was Christopher Wren, a young professor of astronomy and amateur architect, and the last three were nominees of the City Corporation. The new houses, with their bold frontages, relieved of all bays, jutties and other excrescences, expressed in simple form the ideas of the designers.

From 1666 no man in London could plan his own house, for its lay-out, dimensions and proportions were dictated to him by the terms of the Rebuilding Act. The four types of houses prescribed were the models for at least the next fifty years. The first and smallest was the two-storey house with cellar and garret, designed to be put in side streets and lanes; the second was the three-storey house fronting "streets and lanes of note" and the river; the third, the house in the main street of four storeys, and the fourth the "merchant's mansion house of the greatest bigness of four storeys only, and not to be built close to the street front".

The width of streets, an important factor in housing, was also decided by the Commission. Alleys were to be at least 16 ft. in width, and the narrowest throughfares 25-30 ft. This in modern eyes is narrow enough, but it was a great improvement on medieval conditions. Other regulations made later concerned drainage, prohibiting gutters which spouted water

over the roadway and making fall-pipes compulsory, trans-
ferring paving and street cleaning and levelling from the
parishes to a special body of commissioners, and separating the
footway from the carriageway by posts. These provisions
concern the English home only indirectly but were important
to the convenience and personal comfort of the Londoners.
Though they covered only the two square miles of the
devastated City, they provided a model for growing towns to
follow at a later day, and in them we see the origins of the
modern sidewalk, the cambered roadway with underground
drainage and many other common features of home and
street life.

How the ideas of Inigo Jones influenced the planners of
London's new housing may be seen from plans and pictures.
Cellars and garrets were not counted in the two, three or four
storeys, but Londoners had been used for more than a century
to living in them, and hardly one new house was built without
both. The cellars, however, were not true cellars, but basements usually only two-thirds to three-quarters of their height
below ground level, and the tops of the small windows which
let in the light could be seen above ground. The front door of
the house, a few feet above ground level was reached by a
flight of four to six steps and led into a "piano rialzato" or
raised floor where the living-rooms would be. The doorway
was framed within pilasters or engaged columns, and may
have had a hood; the windows were plain and square and the
low-pitched roof was wholly or partly hidden by a brick
parapet or the upper continuation of the brick outer wall, and
behind it the water collected in a leaden channel to be con-
veyed down a fall pipe.

One of the features of the new London was the terrace—a
continuous line of houses either identical or in successive
symmetrical couples. From the beginning, necessity had dictated the joining together of houses, but this had been entirely
haphazard and without system except in certain instances such
as almshouses and in certain places such as Chester, where the

Rows, rebuilt after the fire of 1278, showed some characteristics of terrace building. It was a natural development for the row to be replaced by the terrace, and the idea was later taken up by the high-class architect in places like Bath, Scarborough and the West, as well as the textile employer, mine-owner and the speculative builder of the nineteenth-century suburb.

The Act went into details as to the height of rooms, of cellars and garrets, and the thickness of brickwork for each storey. No wood was to be used on the outside of any house, though oak might be incorporated into shop fronts. The interior of a house was as plain as the exterior, with a narrow hallway and a simple stairway leading to the upper rooms. Provided a builder adhered to the prescribed plan of the house and did not interfere with the structure, he was at liberty to add decorative details in what materials he pleased, and to vary the treatment of doorways, windows, eaves and balconies in any way, while in shop fronts endless variety was possible.

To study the appearance of these houses in London, or in any other town for that matter, one needs to go no further than the works of William Hogarth. Born in 1697, Hogarth sketched life as he saw it. Three-storey buildings are to be seen in the background of his *Beer Street*, with steeply pitched roofs and small garret windows. The other windows are made up of square panes, no longer leaded, but fixed in wooden glazing bars. In the reign of William of Orange the sash was introduced from Holland and this made it possible to slide the parts of the window up and down. A four-storey building, with spectators leaning out of the sash windows, may be seen in the *March to Finchley* (1745), while others may be seen in *The Times of Day* at Covent Garden, Hog Lane and Charing Cross. Hogarth is rich in interiors, one of the most striking of which, *The Poet in Misery*, shows the interior of a miserable garret where the poet sits racking his brains beside the dormer window while his wife mends his breeches, the milk woman at the door demands payment and the stray dog steals the joint from the chair.

The housing which the Rebuilding Commission provided was far better and safer than that which had existed before the Fire, but the best of streets can develop into slums. White-friars, which lay between Fleet Street and the Thames, had never been a choice neighbourhood. Since it had enjoyed the right of sanctuary both before and after the Reformation it had for ages attracted the most disreputable characters. The rebuilding made no difference, for the right of sanctuary was not taken away until the reign of William III (1689-1701) and by that time the district had time to recover its old atmosphere of crime, squalor and vice. It remained the haunt of footpads, pickpockets and highwaymen all through the eighteenth century.

The decline in the tone of any neighbourhood may be traced to a variety of causes, among which are the coming of sea or river traffic through the building of quays and docks, the establishment of offensive industries in the vicinity, the exclusion of a community from the privileges enjoyed by its neighbours, the attractions of illicit gain by robbing the rich, as at Westminster, or the proximity of a prison. One or more of all these factors may contribute, but the evil is increased or even made possible by overcrowding.

This has always been inevitable in cities. Here, where there was not room to have one house to a family, the only way was to build upwards. Or, when the inhabitants of a large house left for a more salubrious neighbourhood, to split it up between several families as was done in London in the six-teenth century when four-storey blocks were common. The usual practice was for one family to live on one floor (hence the word "flat"), all using the common staircase, so that, as a visitor to Elizabethan England put it, most of them seemed to spend their lives hopping up and down from one perch to another like birds in a cage.

To the person of today, accustomed to twentieth-century convenience, tenement life of three hundred years ago must appear unbearable—no water laid on, but all to be fetched from a common tap or pump in a courtyard; no hot water but what was heated on the fire, the nearest sanitation an outside privy used by two or more families, and indoors a vessel which had to be emptied after use; the senses offended by a variety of objectionable smells from inside and outside, and the ears by continual noise. During the day, the bustle of neighbours, street cries and the voices of children, all night long the watchmen crying the hours, footsteps of nightwalkers and voices in the street. But to the tenement-dweller continual exposure to smell and noise made them pass almost unnoticed, and for all its disadvantages life was close and neighbourly. Quarrels and rows there undoubtedly were, for when people live in close proximity feelings come very near to the surface, but the tenement-dweller at least did not suffer from twentieth-century loneliness. The greatest evil was when overcrowding made a reasonable standard of health and cleanliness impossible, when as it is expressed, a whole district "went down" as did Seven Dials, dragging the erstwhile respectable inhabitants with it and laying it open to the inroads of every criminal type.

Seventeenth-century developments in architecture could not fail to be seen in the small and medium-sized detached house, whether in town or country. Italian ideas were enough to give grace and dignity while the English architects still preserved the plainness and solidity of the building. The house was a single block, the larger house had a central entrance hall and staircase, and to make room for it the chimneys were at the ends, the stacks rising from the base of the hipped roof. In the smaller houses one pair of rooms was cut off so that the hall came to one side, the reception room on the other. Towards the end of the century small elaborations were added such as the truncated hipped roof, sometimes with an iron railing surrounding the level space at the top which made it possible for those who lived there to enjoy the view and the fresh air by climbing a narrow stair out of the garret. More elaborate dormer windows with hipped roofs, gables and even curved roofs came into fashion, and the builders of rather larger houses imitated their betters in having that part of the front containing the door and the centre upper window projecting under a triangular pediment. Door ornaments became more elaborate, with projecting canopies, small pediments and semi-circular hoods often worked inside to represent a shell. Doors were solid-looking, with six or eight panels, windows rectangular, the arches and the jambs of bright red brick with keystones, plain or carved. Bricks were now laid in a different way. The old English Bond, in which a line of "headers" was followed by a line of "stretchers" was commonly replaced by the new "Flemish Bond", in which alternate headers and stretchers followed each other in the same line. Though English Bond is the strongest known, Flemish Bond was preferred because it gave a more even and pleasing pattern to the outside of the building.

By this time the smaller house had taken such a well-defined shape that it was no longer necessary, as in the case of the mansion, to have it specially planned by an architect. Most of the post-Fire houses of London had been put up by speculative builders who not only laid the bricks but also employed their own tilers, plumbers, plasterers and carpenters. The best known of these builders was Nicholas Barbon, son of the famous "Praise-God Barebones" after whom one of Cromwell's parliaments was named. He erected hundreds of houses in an about London, varying from the humbler ones around Charing Cross to more stylish ones in St. James's. The plan was simple—one single block or a straightforward row of terrace houses all alike. The only variations were in major matters such as the pitch of the roof, depending mainly on the weight of the tiles or slates used; the positions and designs of chimneys, and in minor matters of decoration and ornament. Thus it was possible for a speculative builder to follow the changing fashion of the day, which was commonly set by the architect who designed the larger houses.

The possibility of varying the ornamentation of houses was now infinite. The late seventeenth century saw the introduc-

Eighteenth-century elaboration: hipped roof, dormers,
pillars and pediments in an ornamental setting. Cornwell
House, Cornwell, Oxfordshire

tion, where the wall joined the roof, of a moulding called the cornice. In larger houses it usually covered the lead guttering and was sometimes made thick enough to hide part of the roof. In the smaller ones, to avoid the expense of buying lead, it was fitted under the eaves. Over the cornice was the garret storey with its dormers, and in some houses the wall was extended upwards above the cornice to form a sort of parapet on which the bottoms of the dormer windows rested, or even into which they were built. This brought the garret into the main body of the house, separated from the rest of the facade only by the decorated line of the cornice. Another new fashion was the reintroduction of the bay, which had been absent since Elizabethan times. In the later years of the century variations of the bay appeared in the bow window and the barrel window.

The greatest revolution made inside the house was brought about by the increased use of wood and iron. England's supplies of timber had now dwindled to such an extent that it could no longer be used as a universal building material. The joists of new houses were therefore of softer wood, imported principally from the Continent, and this was even used in places for wainscoting. In the earlier part of the century ornamentally carved fireplaces were made of wood, but were mainly of marble during the Regency period. By this time a means of smelting iron with coke had been invented and iron-work came to take a more and more prominent place in the household. Iron plates, sometimes decorated with designs in relief, had long been in use for the backs of fireplaces, because bricks tended to disintegrate under the heat. Andirons were no longer used in the smaller fireplaces but were supplanted by ornamental fire-baskets with spikes to prevent logs rolling off if coal was not used. In smaller rooms the firebasket some-times carried a hob on which to stand a pan or kettle. A growing use of iron in the latter part of the period was for the staircase, which could be worked into handsome geometrical curves far more easily than timber, and the steps could be made so that no single one was parallel to those above and below it. In Regency times the staircase maker was a highly skilled craftsman. Bay windows were now running the full height of the building and often had balconies with ornamental iron railings.

Great refinements, especially in ornamentation during this century, were made by the brothers Robert and James Adam. Their work was almost entirely done for wealthier patrons but their designs soon became universal. They introduced a delicacy into both architectural and interior decoration. Even today the Adam interior with its graceful curves, niches and arches, its tasteful if conventional decoration, its soft pastel shades and its delicate furnishings is easily recognisable. Robert Adam was especially successful in his use of composition and "stucco", both inside and outside. Coming at a period when the Wars of the French Revolution and Napoleon limited the supply of bricks, this came in very useful for the builder, especially the man who wished to cover up an imperfect facade. It was generally used only for the ground floor of a building, on which it was scored to represent stone, and moulded into pilasters and other ornaments. The Adam brothers' work was so popular that many of the newly-risen middle classes paid to have their houses and rooms "adamized".

The seventeenth-century nobility were not long in realizing the usefulness of the terrace house. As early as 1631 the Earl of Bedford was granted a licence to develop the open land at Covent Garden for housing. Here, with the help of Inigo Jones, he made the first of all the London squares with houses on three sides, and extending westwards towards St. Martin's-in-the-Fields. This was one of the first essays into town planning in England and being strictly residential it attracted the aristocracy and the wealthier merchants, becoming a very select neighbourhood. It had many advantages: it was open, it stood away from less desirable properties, it was self-contained and it had a centre–the square which was laid out with paths and provided with seats. It was, in fact, a com-

munity project. In their morning walks in the square the
inhabitants got to know one another, and this community
feeling was fostered by the building of a church, designed by
Inigo Jones and started in 1633. The Earl urged his architect
not to go to too great expense, that "he would not have it
much better than a barn". "Well," replied Jones, "you shall
have the handsomest barn in England." The church of St.
Paul was made a parish church in 1645 and in 1671 the market
was set up for the buying and selling "all manner of fruits,
flowers, roots and herbs whatsoever, and also liberty to make
cellars and shops". This early venture had a great influence,
not only on the shape of the future London, but on the kind of
house that was to be built there.

This atmosphere of the small select community was very
much to the taste of London's upper classes, and the project
was followed by others, such as St. James's from 1661 and
Soho from 1672, both by the Earl of St. Albans, and Blooms-
bury in 1664 by the Earl of Southampton, all of which later
became parishes. One outstanding feature of all these was the
terrace house. This was and continued to be the ideal *pied-à-
terre* for the wealthier family who wanted a small, convenient
residence in town or spa, close enough to one's own kind to
be neighbourly, small enough to be cosy, but large enough for
homely intimate receptions, and within easy reach of public
gardens, theatres and baths. The terrace house was economical
in the use of ground space and was in its own way as functional
as the cottage.

To this kind of terrace house it was possible to add any sort
of refinement inside and outside that the architect could
devise. It was possible even to group them together into a
single architectural unit—another aspect of planning. This was
developed by the Adam brothers and others of their time and
was perfected by the Regency architects, of whom the most
important was John Nash. Their compositions vary from the
uniform treatment of a row of houses with imposing doorways, railed areas in front of the basements, in which the eye

A single architectural unit: Park Crescent, off Marylebone
Road, London

falls first on the single units, recognising them as separate
houses, to the very perfection of terrace construction typified
by the Royal Crescent at Bath, the development of Regency
Brighton and Nash's Regent's Park terraces. In these the eye
sees the construction, not as separate houses but rather as a
whole. This was made easier by the hard stucco which Nash
used to such a great extent that the *Quarterly Review* could
print of his work:

> *Augustus of Rome was for building renown'd*
> *And of Marble he left what of brick he had found;*
> *But is not our Nash, too, a very great master?*
> *For he found us all brick, and he leaves us all plaster.*

Nevertheless, the uniformity achieved by building plane surfaces in imitation of expanses of Bath stone gave them the appearance of the "palazzo". This was fully realised and a condition of the lease of the Regent's Park terraces was the four-yearly repainting of the stone, wood and iron of the terraces and the repair and re-colouring of the stucco, "the colour of such stucco not to be varied or changed at any time but always to be in imitation of Bath stone". The plan of the terrace house was fundamentally the same as that of the London re-building, with two rooms on each floor, these for the family, i.e. the living room and the parlour on the ground floor; on the first the drawing-rooms where receptions were held, and above, the bedrooms. The hall in these houses, with its stair-case at one end and the front door at the other, tended to be dark. A certain amount of light entered by the landing window and from a small pane which was inserted above the front door. This panel was usually semi-circular and the bars radiated from the middle of the base line. For this reason, whether fan-shaped or not, it has since been called a fanlight.

At the rear of the house were the coach-houses or stables. The servants lived in the basement and slept in the garrets, which often had a separate stair. Later, the space under the pavement was dug out and used as a coal store, the coal being shot through a hole in the pavement covered by an iron grate.

In the late eighteenth century England entered on the period of development which eventually transformed it from a predominantly agricultural to an industrial country. This was accompanied by a rapid growth of population in towns where manufacturers were concentrated, and a corresponding demand for housing. The terrace house answered them all. It had been as suitable for London's urban development as for the needs of the small upper-class colony. In the absence of efficient control over building, water supply and drainage, it was subsequently to take more sinister forms when it became the prevailing type of dwelling in the factory districts.

VIII

Darkest England

In the early nineteenth century the increasing variety of industrial products and the concentration of much wealth in few hands gave to the British aristocrat and industrial magnate a standard of magnificent living that was known and envied everywhere.

For this a price had to be paid in the decay of local industry and craftsmanship. The same turnpike roads on which the Flying Post sped with the latest news from town to town, the network of canals which could transport their tons of bricks, coal, timber and ironware from one end of the country to another, and especially the railway which after 1840 opened up districts previously almost inaccessible, were the first means of supplying cheap goods of uniform stamp to all parts of the country and bringing about a greater uniformity of material and structure. From this point of view it became easier, for the middle classes at least, to ape, with cheaper products, the luxuries enjoyed by the rich.

The social historian has stated with good reason that in the age before all this happened, the eighteenth century, England presented a variety both in building styles and local crafts, and an excellence in hand-produced goods not equalled since that time. In the case of the English home, this is true, for in the nineteenth century the greater production of bricks, the migration of large numbers of people to the new towns and the erection by the speculative builders of thousands of mean and ill-equipped terrace houses helped to create not only Cobbett's hated London "Wen" but a number of others of the same kind in every industrial centre in the country. Though for the rich this was indeed a period of luxury, for the poor hardly any age can surpass it in misery, want and degradation.

Below the aristocracy, which enjoyed a special place at the apex of the pyramid of society, were a number of classes which though distinct in themselves merged imperceptibly one into another. The substantial farmer, largely the product of the Age of Enclosure, was paralleled in the towns by the merchant. Below him came the village craftsman, the carpenter, tanner, smith or wheelwright, usually respected for his skill and often occupying the sometimes unenviable position of parish constable or headborough. Corresponding to him in the town was the respectable craftsman, and the growing class of office and clerical workers, many of them copper-plate writers, since the typewriter had not yet been invented. These were the Cratchits of the day, men whose feet echoed morning by morning on the pavements of Somers Town, White-chapel and across London Bridge on the way to work from their drab houses in some street in the nearer suburbs. Poor but proud, they struggled to hold their place in society, but their lot was insecure; a change in employer or a setback in health could so easily cast them down into the ranks of the "respectable poor". Below them came the lowest class of all, the very poor, respectable, workless, shiftless and criminal who in the country inhabited the hovels, by now sadly increased in numbers, and in the town the slums.

The palace of the great nobleman was rather an establishment than a home, but it still had to serve as a home for the regiment of men and women, boys and girls, who staffed it. Of these only the head men had their separate cottages. The outside workers and under-gardeners lived in the bothy, a large communal one-room dwelling, and a woman was specially employed to keep it clean. The indoor servants were housed within the building, except in some cases the laundry-maids who slept in the laundry. Only a few of the servants, the butler and the housekeeper, and possibly the chef, head cook and tutor were allowed their own rooms. The rest had dormitory accommodation in the top storey of the building. During the day they worked downstairs in the basement, wash-house, still-room or kitchen and rarely, if ever, saw their employers. For all but the higher ranks of servants this was but a temporary home; on marriage the men found other jobs and after a period in service both men and women usually drifted into cottage life and, often, penury.

The mansion was a great establishment, but it was without some of the comforts we consider essential to the modern home. There was no bathroom and hot water had to be carried up from basement to bedrooms each morning and poured into a great basin on the hearth for my lord or his lady to enjoy. Water closets were in use, and these drained into cesspools, which were sometimes very close to or even under the building itself. Since the drainage pipes were often badly jointed, and were not glazed until after 1840, bad drains were rather the rule than the exception. The cesspools were often so old and well-used that they were overflowing. Fifty-three such were discovered under Windsor Castle in 1844, and the smell or absence of smell from the drains was often regarded rather as a way of forecasting the weather than as a warning of bad throats or fevers. In London in 1846 there were 200,000 undrained cesspools. Even Queen Victoria's own apartments in Buckingham Palace were ventilated by air entering through the common sewer. In 1871 Edward VII contracted typhoid as a result, it is said, of a visit to a mansion in Yorkshire. Naturally the poor suffered most from this state of affairs, but no class was entirely exempt from the dangers.

One of the chief features of the age was the change in the place of residence of the producing classes. The farmer, who had once thought it necessary himself to live in the old half-timbered or stone-built farmhouse which his family had inhabited for generations, preferred to build himself a new one of brick, and the old one he split up into smaller lots for his labourers, the wings for one family each and the centre part, or hall, for a third. The town merchant bought a house in the country, sometimes even purchased a manor and ran it as a business concern, living there part of the year and drawing quitrents from his copyholders. The shopkeeper whose father had lived in the rooms above his shop let them and turned the shop into a lock-up, taking one of the newer houses farther away from the city centre. This district, once always vibrant with life and movement, became almost dead during the night except for a few caretakers and the odd remaining residents. In London, which serves as an example, the area thus affected was one part of the city itself. It has spread in this century far beyond the confines of the old city walls.

Conditions in the town mansion were far worse for the servants than in the country house. Basements, often almost entirely below ground level, had to be lit artificially and their occupants saw the light of day only during their brief off-periods. Even the butlers' and housekeepers' rooms were often located there, for want of space, while the workrooms were in the garrets where the servants slept. Since there were no sewing-machines, the stitches in the elaborate dresses worn by fashionable women had to be done by hand.

If he could afford it the businessman or shopkeeper had a villa built for himself on the town's outskirts to suit his own tastes. The locality no longer dictated the style or the materials of the building, for transport had made available almost anything he wanted. It was possible for him to build in inferior brick and then hide everything with a coat of elaborately decorated *stucco duro*. His architects could provide him with specimens and details of every style; the gables and false timbers of mock Tudor, the Romanesque with its pillared portico, arched windows and pediment, the straight and severe lines of Greece, the shallow roof and regular uniform windows of the Italian style or the heavy-pillared porch and balconied bay of the Regency. Many of the features, brick-nogging, leaded lights, porticoes, ostentatious Tudor chimneys and cornices were not essential to the buildings.

The interiors, at least until after the Great Exhibition of 1851, remained predominantly Georgian, but changes were already creeping in and 1851 accelerated the process. Oil and colza lamps gave way to gas in the towns; wallpaper, especially after the repeal of the tax, became almost universal. The piano, once very rare, was now a necessary article of furniture in the refined household.

It was in the middle-class household more than anywhere else that the extravagance and ornamentation of Victorian furnishing was predominant, for many of the middle-class were newly rich, unencumbered by family heirlooms and antiques. Therefore they exploited to the full their taste for the mock Greek, Elizabethan, French and Dutch Renaissance, the ornaments of white and gilt, the fancy work-tables, pier-glasses, circular dining tables, sparkling glass chandeliers, papier maché screens, musical boxes, whatnots, fruits and flowers under glass globes, heavy gold-ornamented curtains and thick multicoloured carpets. The all-over effect was impressive, but showed little consideration for the poor slavey condemned to a lifetime of dusting and scrubbing.

In some parts of England, especially the Midlands, where enclosure had first robbed the smallholders of their common rights and then forced large numbers to give up their land and with it their independence, life in cottages underwent a sad transformation. Their occupants, forced back on relief, were in no condition to resist the pressure from above. Evictions, the loss of the woman's domestic industry, the supplementing of wages from the poor rate, and finally the Act of 1834 abolishing out-relief to the able-bodied and forcing whole families into the dreaded Union workhouse, demoralised the agricultural population and struck a heavy blow at the old-fashioned cottage economy of rural England. Cobbett saw it when he toured England in 1830. Fifteen years later Disraeli described it graphically in his novel *Sybil*:

"With the exception of the dull high street, which had the usual characteristics of a small agricultural market town, some sombre mansions, a dingy inn, and a petty bourse, Marney mainly consisted of a variety of narrow and

crowded lanes formed by cottages built of rubble, or un-
hewn stones without cement, and from age, or badness of
the material, looking as if they could scarcely hold together.
The gaping chinks admitted every blast; the leaning
chimneys had lost half their original height; the rotten
rafters were evidently misplaced; while in many instances
the thatch, yawning in some parts to admit the wind and
wet, and in all utterly unfit for its original purpose of giving
protection from the weather, looked more like the top of a
dunghill than a cottage. Before the doors of these dwellings,
and often surrounding them, ran open drains full of animal
and vegetable refuse, decomposing into disease, or sometimes in their imperfect course filling foul pits or spreading
into stagnant pools, while a concentrated solution of every
species of dissolving filth was allowed to soak through and
thoroughly impregnate the walls and ground adjoining."

Conditions were becoming even worse in the rapidly filling industrial towns where accommodation had to be found
for the influx of people from the countryside seeking work.
Some employers took on the work of house-building on their
own account, and round the imposing factory gates small
networks of mean streets arose, creating a sort of community
which soon had its pub and generally one or more non-
conformist chapels. In other cases the erection of dwellings
was left to the speculative builder who put them up as cheaply
as possible and had his income from the rents he drew. The
Hammonds quote an account of how this happened in
Bradford:

"An individual who may have a couple of thousand
pounds does not exactly know what to do with it, having
no occasion for it in trade; he wishes to lay it out so as to
pay him the best percentage in money; he will purchase a
plot of ground, an acre or half an acre; then what he thinks
about, is to place as many houses on this acre of ground as
he possibly can, without reference to drainage or anything, except that which will pay him a good percentage

Late 19th-century terrace houses in Lambeth. At the rear of each house is a kitchen with separate chimney, lean-to scullery and small back garden. Pantiles are a common feature of these roofs

for his money; that is the way in which the principal part of the suburbs of Bradford has sprung up."[1]

The overall plan was the same in other cities, varying only in small details. In Manchester the construction was superficial and there were no cellars; in Bradford, where sandstone was plentiful, the houses were more substantially built, with cellars lit by low windows peeping a few inches above street level and a square iron plate fixed low on the outer wall which could be detached when coal was to be shot. Leeds presented a monotonous vista of dull red brick relieved only by tower-

[1] *The Bleak Age,* by J. L. and B. Hammond (Pelican, 1947)

ing mill chimneys which belched smoke, and by the needle-like spires of churches. In Halifax might be seen the underground "cellar kitchen" which was normally used as a living room, while in Lancashire the tendency was towards a much flimsier construction with no cellars at all. In Newcastle and the north-east there was more splitting up of old properties and conversion into tenements. Everywhere, small irregular spaces were filled in with innumerable courts, sometimes joined together by narrow alleys known as "ginnels" or "snickets", about a yard in width, running between the high walls of houses, twisting and turning between the blocks, unpaved and unlit. Of the latter, Nottingham, where space was severely limited, was an outstanding example.

It is in a way surprising that in books of antiquarians, written at the turn of the century, there appears little evidence of the desparate conditions that prevailed in many localities. Descriptions of sordid alleys, holes and corners of towns, even when illustrated by pen-drawings, give little idea of the filth and vermin that existed there. Some even go into mild heroics extolling the grit and endurance of their forbears in managing to live and to draw a certain amount of merriment out of their lot. Only in the odd song or poem, usually in dialect, do we get a faint glimpse of the black side of the cloud. The full impact of industry on town and home life had to wait for realisation until the social historian, fortified by his researches into contemporary records, produced a truer and more balanced picture.

Conditions in some parts of London were little better; visitors to the Great Exhibition of 1851 who saw only the select squares of the West End and Kensington knew little of the misery in some of the London parishes. Dickens described it in 1836 *(Sketches by Boz)* in the melancholy recital of Mr. Bung, the Broker's Man:

"I was once put into a house down George's Yard–that little dirty court at the back of the gasworks; and I shall never forget the misery of them people, dear me! . . . .

There was only two rooms in the house, and as there was no passage, the lodgers upstairs always went through the room of the people of the house, as they passed in and out . . . . There was a little piece of enclosed dust in front of the house with a cinder-path leading up to the door, and an open rain-water butt on one side. A dirty striped curtain, on a very slack string, hung in the window, and a little triangular bit of looking-glass rested on the sill inside . . . . There was two or three chairs, that might have been worth, in their best days, from eightpence to a shilling apiece; a small deal table, an old corner cupboard with nothing in it, and one of these bedsteads which turn up half-way, and leave the bottom legs sticking out for you to knock your head against, or hang your hat upon; no bed, no bedding. There was an old sack, by way of a rug, before the fireplace, and four or five children were grovelling about among the sand on the floor."

His descriptions of Jacob's Island (*Oliver Twist,* 1838) and the "black dilapidated street" known as Tom-all-Alone's (*Bleak House,* 1852) are not creations of the imagination, but cold statements of fact. Both expose slum conditions in London in all their horror. On Jacob's Island

". . . a stranger, looking from one of the wooden bridges thrown across it at Mill Lane, will see the inhabitants of the houses on either side lowering from their back doors and windows, buckets, pails, domestic utensils of all kinds, in which to haul the water up: and when his eye is turned from these operations to the houses themselves, his utmost astonishment will be excited by the scene before him. Crazy wooden galleries common to the backs of half-a-dozen houses, with holes from which to look upon the slime beneath; windows broken and patched, with poles thrust out, on which to dry the linen that is never there; rooms so small, so filthy, so confined, that the air would seem too tainted even for the dirt and squalor which they shelter; wooden chambers thrusting themselves out above the mud, and threatening to fall into it, as some have done; dirt-besmeared walls and decaying foundations; every repulsive lineament of poverty, every loathsome indication of filth, rot, and garbage; all these ornament the banks of Folly Ditch."

Peter Cunningham, Author of the *Handbook of London,* discovered in 1849 in Portman Square a court 22 ft. wide, surrounded by 26 three-storey houses in which lived 914 people. The only drainage was a common sewer running through the court. In 1846 Lord Morpeth, the Whig reformer, asked his hearers if they had ever "tracked the swarm of human life, of decrepit age, of blighted manhood and of stunted infancy into the steaming and reeking receptacles of filth and fever, and every kind of loathsomeness, into which they are but too often stuffed and crammed—and this too, within a stone's throw of your own most luxurious dwellings, in the near neighbourhood of the gaudiest theatres, of the halls of legislators and of the shrines of religion."

These were old decaying properties, but conditions were not much better in some of the new ones. The opening of the Eastern counties Railway (1839) and other lines, the Stratford Railway Works (1846) and the construction of the Victoria Dock (1850–55) brought about a rapid increase of population east of the River Lea. In the north of West Ham parish, streets of substantial Victorian houses were built, but in other parts near the river Lea and the new docks, a rash of mean and insanitary dwellings soon covered the marshland. In a little-known report to the General Board of Health (1855) on the sanitary conditions in the parish, the Superintending Inspector, Alfred Dickens, described the terrible conditions in some of these streets and courts. Of Wood's Yard near the High Street in Stratford, Dickens says:

"There are ten houses here; they are built of wood, and the level of the floor is generally below the surface of the ground. The yard is unpaved and dirty. Surface very uneven and irregular. There is a privy in the end house in a

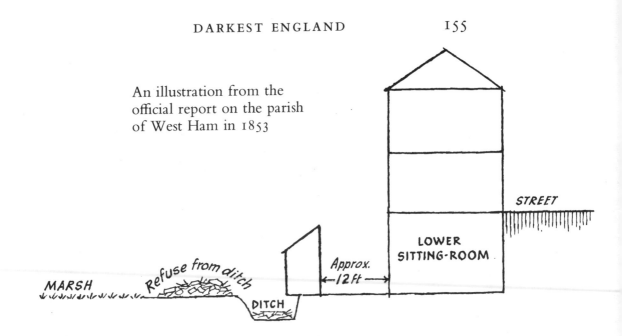

An illustration from the official report on the parish of West Ham in 1853

STREET

LOWER SITTING-ROOM

Approx. ←12 ft→

MARSH Refuse from ditch

DITCH

room under a sleeping apartment. Mr. Duck informed me this was used, to all intents and purposes, as a public privy. It is in a most foul and filthy condition, and smells most offensive. The tenant of the cottage (Mrs. Applethwaite) says the smell in the bedroom is almost unbearable, and her children have frequently suffered from it. She pays three shillings a week for the house, which contains three rooms besides the place the privy is in. Another house in the court contains only one room in which four persons reside. The water is laid on from the East London Water Works into a tub. It is turned on in the morning for a short time only about long enough to fill the tub, which is uncovered and in a very dirty condition. The water, said to be pretty good as it comes from the pipe, is very dirty in the tub, and yet must be used for drinking and other household purposes, the people having no other supply."

The water for another court had to be carried from a neighbouring hostelry. Here the houses were no more than mere hovels; one had only one room, furnished with a broken chair and a heap of rags for a bed. It was tenanted by a man

North-country alley, Birkenhead, with small backyards opening on to it. The brick out-buildings are water closets and much of the remaining garden space is taken up with sheds etc.

who had two large dogs. Another had a privy in the back kitchen which was emptied only four times a year. In a row of tenements abutting on one of the many ditches, the backs of the houses were a full eight feet below street level and at the end of the yard, only twelve feet from the back doors, the privy overhung the ditch which, with refuse piled up on the opposite bank, "stank abominably". Such was the nineteenth century English home at its worst.

The building of terraces had come to stay. The better class terrace house had its narrow hall, sometimes in the north called a passage, out of which rose the flight of stairs, cased in and lit by a first-storey window at the top. An equally narrow landing opened out to two bedrooms. In many houses another wooden, boxed-in staircase led to the large one-room attic lit by one or more skylights, high in the roof with no dormers. On the ground floor were usually two rooms, the living-rooms at the back of the house, and the "best room" or parlour at the front. The living-room opened near the back door on to a "cellar-head" which had its own small window with, under or alongside it, the only water supply the house possessed, a single cold water tap over a stone sink. From the cellar-head a flight of stairs, usually brick or stone, led to the cellar. This was usually divided into two parts, a keeping cellar and, shut off from it, the coal cellar into which a thin pencil of light penetrated through the chinks in the grate at road level.

There was no bathroom but in the cellar was usually kept the large metal bath which was used at set times by various members of the family. The floor of the living room was sometimes bare, sometimes laid with patterned oilcloth worn through in places, especially near the door and around the white-topped deal table. In front of the hearth was the home-made rug, made of small "tabs" of waste cloth pricked into a canvas backing in patterns of coloured circles, squares and diamonds. Making such a rug was undertaken by the whole family when enough clean rags had been collected. Whole evenings were spent over the frame and the laying of the rug when finished was a family event. The only cooking facility was the fire, on one side of which was the oven and on the other usually a "set pan", both part of the iron range. In the pan it was possible, when the fire was lit, to keep a continuous if meagre supply of warm water. This came in handy when the bath was brought up and placed on the rug in front of the fire for the family ablutions.

Sanitation was still primitive. From the kitchen sink a leaden pipe ran down through the outer wall to an outdoor sink through which dirty water trickled through a soakaway, either into a cesspool or into the local drainage system. Other inside sanitation there was none, but outside the house at the back was the privy, a square or rectangular cabin of brick or stone with two large flat slabs of sandstone, one overlying the other, as a roof. On one of its sides was the door by which it was entered; on the other was a smaller opening, usually about waist high covered by a wooden latched door. This the scavenger opened on emptying days and with his shovel entered to throw out the refuse which was taken away in carts and stored, since it was highly valued as manure to be scattered over the fields on the outskirts of the town.

People who lived under such conditions in 1850 were indeed fortunate, for the majority were far worse off. A group of terrace houses in Preston, condemned by a Royal Commission on sanitary grounds, was built in two rows, the backs separated by small yards, each one about half the area covered by the house. The back door was not more than about seven feet from an earth closet, the sewage from which flowed into an open sewer which ran between the two lines of yards and from there flowed into a cesspool. The cesspool was emptied by the landlord only twice a year and the contents sold for manure. Living conditions in houses such as these, especially as pigs were kept in the small yards, beggar the imagination. Yet there were many such.

Even these houses had the advantage of back and front doors, which so many others lacked, for this was the age of the back-to-back house, a type of construction to be seen even today all over the north of England. Two rows face each other, but each row contains two rows of dwellings within itself, one row facing the street and the other opening on to enclosed courtyards. The houses are usually grouped in fours— No. 2 (rear) behind No. 1 (front); No. 4 (rear) behind No. 3 (front). Between 2–1 and 4–3 is an enclosed passage from street to yard, running under two bedrooms, in order that the occupants of 1 and 3 might have access to the privies at the back.

In spite of the lack of a through current of air, back-to-back housing need not be unhealthy, for there are many blocks standing today in open situations, without the typical passage, each house with its own small garden and cabin, that

Late 19th-century back-to-back houses in Bradford. A feature of their interior construction was the large living-room. Stairways linked kitchen with cellar and living-room with a small landing and two bedrooms

are both convenient and healthy. But for the most part back-to-back housing combined with a limited water supply and defective drainage was the rule. In many instances water was not laid on but had to be fetched from a pump which supplied a whole unit, and often enough the same unit was provided with only one, two or three privies. To keep a certain amount of privacy the families which used each one were supplied with identical keys. Such an arrangement never worked and invariably resulted in excessive and disagreeable use of the chamber-pot.

The frontage of the back-to-back house is divided between kitchen and living-room in the rough proportion of about two-thirds to one-third, each room having a separate window. The entrance door leads directly into the living-room and the entrance is alongside the wall of the kitchen into which, about four feet from the entrance door, another leads off. In the kitchen by the window is the sink, and at the rear of the kitchen a steep flight of steps, twisting at the bottom, leads from the cellar-head into the cellars. All stairs are steep, and because of the shortage of space sometimes twist at the top before reaching the landing leading to the two bedrooms. Some back-to-back houses have a second wooden boxed-in stair leading to attics which have the usual skylight window.

The houses backing on to each other are symmetrical in construction. Those facing the street have no gardens, but the occupants of those facing the courtyards have in some cases boldly torn up the brick paving or stone slabs and created beauty in the most unpropitious surroundings. A few have even built themselves small greenhouses.

It is most difficult to treat these houses as part of history, for though they are now being taken down by progressive local authorities in their thousands, almost all possess one uniform feature–the drab, purple-grey roof of Welsh slate. This roofing material was introduced into England in the late eighteenth century and its fissile qualities, for it can be split into extremely thin sheets, give it the advantage of light weight and therefore easy carriage. A roof bearing it need not therefore have such stout rafters. Laid in courses of diminishing sizes or in patterns, Welsh slates could be made to look well, but nobody gave much thought to looks when housing the poor.

Overcrowding brought a host of evils in its train. Refuse was at first disposed of by sale to neighbouring farmers, but as the town grew larger, the amount of sewage deposited increased beyond the powers of the local authority to deal with it. Cartage to more distant farms destroyed any profit arising from it; tipping it become objectionable and collection was neglected. Washing it into the soil was no remedy. Streams running through towns, once clean and inhabited by fish became polluted and stinking. Bradford's drainage and industrial refuse poured into one such stream earned it the name of "T'mucky Beck". Street cleaning was neglected and whole streets were left swimming in filth, sometimes for six months. Water, scarce enough at the best of times, became contaminated through the seepings of cesspools and graveyards; flies, which were not at this time thought to have any connection with disease, were allowed to live and breed; the film of black smoke constantly overhanging the industrial city penetrated the lungs, causing more coughs and catarrhs, and often what light got through was prevented from entering some parts of a house as a result of the Window Tax. This tax, imposed in 1696 and repealed in 1851, affected houses with more than eight windows, but was levied for even the smallest opening and was made an excuse for leaving privies, passages, cellars and roofs unventilated. Add to all this streets brimming with filth, unpaved or badly paved, broken and rutted by the passage of heavy carts, the throngs of children at a time when the birthrate was higher than ever before, the problem of drink when as a result of the Act of 1828 beer for the consumption off the premises could be sold without a licence, and life in the streets of an English manufacturing town must have been more sordid than anything Dickens ever wrote about the London of his day.

Comparison between the conditions of working people in the poorer agricultural areas and the industrial towns are hard to come by. In July 1832, the Reverend George Stringer Bull, the campaigner for the Ten Hours Bill to restrict the working day of children in factories, in evidence before a Committee of Parliament, stated that although the labourers in his native county of Essex had lower wages (8s. as compared with 12s. in the textile industry), their lot was far better. They paid less in rent, had fewer expenses and shorter hours, 6 to 6 in summer and 7 to 5 in winter, compared with the 12 to 14 hours regularly worked in a Yorkshire factory. Their housing was better, they had gardens in which they could grow herbs and vegetables, they lived in the open air and had less need of the doctor. But they were still far from the fortunate state of Crabbe's happy cottager.

IX

The Way Out

By the mid-nineteenth century intelligent opinion throughout the country was alive to the perils arising from the town
rookery and the rural slum. Cottage design, the planning of
small settlements for the poor and even town planning came
into fashion. James Silk Buckingham (1786–1855), traveller,
author, Member of Parliament and controversialist, produced
in 1848 a plan for a modern Temperance Community, to
which he gave the name Victoria. Every inhabitant was to be
a shareholder and the town was to be planned on class lines,
the richest people in the largest houses nearest the centre, the
poorest on the outer ring near the workshops. Schools, community halls, recreational centres and churches were to be on
common land. The town was to hold its own courts; education and medicine were to be free to all, smoking and the
drinking of intoxicating liquors were to be forbidden.

Other planners were less utopian and more occupied with
practical schemes. In 1842 the Metropolitan Association for
Improving the Dwellings of the Poor was founded and in
1849 the first block of family dwellings was put up in Deal
Street, Stepney. In these, for the first time, tenement dwellings
for the working classes were given the stamp of respectability.
The blocks, five storeys high, consisted of four-room flats,
living-room, scullery and two bedrooms, approached by outside landings or "streets in the air". Main water was laid on to
the scullery, which had a refuse shoot and a lavatory. For this
Association Prince Albert himself designed a model tenement
block of four flats, for which he was awarded the Gold Medal
Class VII at the Great Exhibition. The flats each had a lobby,
a living-room, a water-closet, a scullery with water laid on, a

Victorian workers' dwellings. Courtyard of New Beacons-
field Buildings, near King's Cross, London, erected by the
Victoria Dwellings Association, 1879

dustshaft and ventilator, a meat safe and coal bin. The three
bedrooms had external ventilation. The cost to build amount-
ed to about £450 per flat, and the rent was 3s. 6d. to 4s. Since
this rent could only be afforded by a skilled worker in constant employment the dwellings hardly contributed at all towards the decrease in slums, but they were a pointer in the
right direction and provided an impetus for others. More
accommodation was provided by George Peabody (1795–
1869), an American merchant who had settled in London and
who gave half a million towards building dwellings for the
working classes. It was spent mainly in the erection of tall,
five-and six-storey tenement blocks. Though these were less
wasteful of space than the two-storey Albert dwellings, they

stood in greater danger of deteriorating into a new kind of slum.

The move towards decent housing for the working classes, inspired by such men as Robert Owen, Richard Elsam and J. B. Papworth after the Napoleonic Wars, took shape in the 'forties, gained momentum in the half century which followed and expressed itself in philanthropic action, collective effort and a vast body of housing and public health legislation. By 1850 the country was emerging from the bleak age of scarcity and repression. The Repeal of the Corn Laws had given a forward urge to British industry which had no competitor on a world market, and, while wages showed no great tendency to rise, the free admission of foreign goods into the country tended to bring prices down and to raise the standard of living. A foreign prince, heartily disliked by hard-headed statesmen and politicians, was nevertheless teaching the English people to be proud of their country. But there were other spurs to action. From 1833 onwards, the dreaded cholera had attacked the population of the urban centres and something had to be done to prevent whole cities being choked with their own filth. London took its first step in the destruction of the disreputable and unsavoury rookery known as Porridge Island which stood between St. Martin's-in-the-Fields and Whitehall. In its place a wide square was laid out and named in memory of the Battle of Trafalgar. Here the Nelson Column was erected in 1843. This and the district around Charing Cross was one of the first of London's great clearances. It was followed by the establishment of the Metropolitan Board of Works in 1855. Between that year and the setting up of the London County Council in 1888 the Board carried out a stupendous reforming policy which resulted in the clearing of many sites, the creation of Shaftesbury Avenue, Queen Victoria Street, the Thames Embankment, New Oxford Street and Charing Cross Road, besides the building of Holborn Viaduct in 1867-9. The expenditure of six and half millions on main drains and the upkeep of nearly three thousand acres of parkland changed the dismal appearance of much of London as Dickens knew it to that of the London of to-day.

The last chapters in the story of the English Home cannot be written without some consideration of the great mass of legislation which brought into being modern standards of housing. The first consideration, the health of the people, had been constantly dwelt on both by the philanthropists and the Poor Law Commissioners. The result was the formation in 1848 of a Board of Health in Whitehall which had the power to supersede the old system of parish control and establish local boards with, among other powers, a certain amount of supervision over housing. Gradually, as one local authority after another adopted the Act, the rash of slums which had spread, especially in the large cities, was checked. The Shaftesbury Act of 1851 enabled towns with more than 10,000 inhabitants to build and put out to rent cheap houses, to acquire land and to borrow from a Public Works Loan Fund to finance their housing ventures. Though this had little effect in the years immediately after its enactment, it became very important once the housing drive had gained momentum at the end of the century. A Nuisance Removal Act of 1855 made provision for the recognition by local authorities of premises "injurious to health" and for prohibiting their habitation. In this Act overcrowding was statutorily recognised as a danger to health and provision was made for curbing it.

By this time the larger municipalities were obtaining private acts to deal with their own problems. The Cross Act of 1875, so named after the Home Secretary of the time, which made provision for the demolition of insanitary areas, was followed by a number of provincial schemes involving the reconstruction of hundreds of acres of property, and in 1890 a Housing of the Working Classes Act followed the report of a Royal Commission of which the Prince of Wales was a member. This urged the continuance of the policy of clearance and backed it up by the offer of loans. Between 1881 and 1905 more than two millions were lent to various local authorities. By the end of the century all local authorities were compelled to secure under their by-laws the proper construction of houses, including measures to prevent damp, to provide good drainage and the removal of refuse, a good water supply and sanitary conveniences as well as the cleaning of streets. They were given the power to inspect and enquire, to compel owners to make good unsound property and, if they failed, to demolish it. An act of 1909 was the last of this long series to be passed before the 1914-18 war.

By this time, though the worst aspects of the slum problem had been tackled, there were still acres upon acres of mean streets and still many courts where lavatory accommodation was insufficient and overcrowding rife. But standards had been evolved, and private agencies had been forced to consider other things besides profit in the erection of houses. Between 1885 and 1905 nearly 10,000 back-to-back houses had been dealt with, of which half had been destroyed and half reconditioned. Great impetus had been given to the construction of lodging houses, block dwellings, tenements, cottage flats and small cottages, many thousands had been built by private enterprise and charitable concerns.

Pioneers in housing continued to keep the subject in the public eye, and of these the chief was Octavia Hill (1838-1912). The family interest in social reform brought her at an early age into contact with the Ragged School Movement and formed in her the conviction that environment had a great influence in making or marring the individual. From that time she put all her energy into a campaign for better housing. Beginning with the purchase of a single, small group of houses in Marylebone the activities of the friends she enrolled as helpers spread until she had many groups under her control and was acting as manager for large property-owning bodies such as the Ecclesiastical Commission. Her object was to discover and cultivate the self-respect of tenants through good organization, clean business dealings, the avoidance of indiscriminate giving and patronage, and above all the fostering of beauty in the home and its surroundings. In comparison with the size of the housing problem the actual work done by Octavia Hill and her sister was small indeed, but their effect on convincing those in power that good housing for the working classes was their right and that it could be created, was enormous.

Among other pioneers were several employers of labour. At a time when population was migrating from the countryside to the towns one way to attract the best workers was to provide them with decent housing. As early as 1776 the family of Strutt had started the manufacture of cotton at Belper in Derbyshire. There and at Milford they built stone houses in terraces with gardens in front and yards at the back, living-room and scullery on the ground floor, two bedrooms, attics and cellars.

Sir Titus Salt, the West Riding wool magnate, went even farther. After having made a fortune principally by the manufacture of mohair and alpaca, he decided to gather all his establishments into one comprehensive whole. The town of Bradford, where most of them were situated, disgusted him with its evil smelling dyke and unhealthy workrooms and cottages. Inspired by the reading of Disraeli's *Coningsby* (1844), he decided to move further downstream into the cleaner atmosphere of the Aire valley beyond Shipley, and there to found his own model settlement. Here he built 800 dwelling-houses of stone covering an area of 26 acres, each with parlour, kitchen, pantry and cellar, and at least three bedrooms. Some were designed as boarding-houses for single operatives. All those in the principal streets had front gardens. The twenty-five streets which constituted the village were laid out in straight lines and paved. Every need of the inhabitants was catered for. There were 42 almshouses, schoolrooms, baths, wash-houses, a literary institute, churches and a fourteen-acre park pleasantly sloping towards the river Aire. The comment of a modern authority–"rows of rather crowded, grim houses", is much at variance with the opinion of that day:

> "The estate which received the name of Saltaire by the combination of the name of the founder with that of the river on which the estate is situated . . . has before now been likened to a commercial Utopia. . . . As a town–and especially as a manufacturing town–it is a marvel of cleanliness, cheerfulness and beauty. Its inhabitants should be, whether they are or not, a superior and happy people. With constant work, decent homes, and munificent provision for instruction, amusement and recreation close at hand, we cannot imagine any rational cause for discontent. . . . The dignity of labour is upheld there in its integrity, and 'charity' in its demoralizing sense is unrecognised by the employer or the employed."

The establishment of this community, a brave conception, took almost twenty years, the factory being opened in September 1853 and the park in 1871. Modern views on the effectiveness of Saltaire do not alter the fact that to the neighbouring Bradfordians it must indeed have seemed a Utopia. It was the first and greatest community plan to emerge since Owen's experiment at New Lanark half a century before. Many employers, setting up factories in out-of-the-way places, have since built houses near them, but up to 1914, at least, few followed Salt's example. Among those who did were Lever Brothers (Port Sunlight near Liverpool, 1886), Cadbury's (Bournville near Birmingham, completed 1895) and Sir Joseph Rowntree (Earswick, near York, laid out in 1905). At a time when standards of housing were changing yearly and community development was coming to the fore, these schemes were more elaborate than Salt's had been.

The period leading up to 1914 was one of intense and bitter struggle on the part of the working classes for a better standard of living. Trade Unions found their feet, the Labour Party came into existence and the strike weapon was developed. The coming of universal elementary education and the

A Queen Anne residence with typical Victorian additions.
Ravenswood House, West Wickham, Kent

cheap newspaper helped to produce an articulate working-class whose voice could no longer be ignored as the Acts of 1867 and 1884-5 had given them the parliamentary vote. Moreover, from the eighteen-fifties, their efforts at co-operation had been pursued on a sound basis. Friendly Societies, sick clubs and pig clubs encouraged the thrifty workers to provide for the future. Penny-a-week insurance and burial clubs gave the working-class funeral the pomp that it had never before enjoyed. The existence of housing Societies was made possible by Lord Shaftesbury's Act of 1851. In 1895 the National Housing Reform Council (later the National Housing and Town Planning Council) was set up largely through the efforts of labour groups. By the end of the century the most advanced thinkers—doctors, reformers, philanthropists and all—were looking back on the stark evidence of the sins of their fathers and were unanimous that the fight for sunshine, clean air and pleasant surroundings was to be one of the most important of the coming century. Within fifty years the whole balance of the housing question had completely altered from that of providing decent accommodation for paupers to that of building not only homes but communities for the whole population. Local authorities, fortified by legislation, began to concern themselves about the erection of dwellings for the working-classes, and the voluntary societies functioning on a non-profit basis embarked on housing schemes. By 1901 the Co-operative Societies had already built 25,000 homes in Britain, which when completed were usually bought by their occupants.

One aspect of this latter movement was the conception of the Garden City and the Garden Suburb. The first of these was built by a co-partnership housing society called Ealing Tenants Limited, set up in 1901. This kind of society spread until in 1909 there were twelve. The general procedure of such a body was for the members to pool their capital, then to buy land, and after the houses were built to charge a rent which would return 5% on share capital and 4% on loan capital to each member, until the returns of each one had accumulated to a sum equal to the value of the house he occupied.

The Garden City idea was first put forward by Ebenezer Howard in a book first published in 1898, and the first Garden Suburb was opened near to Hampstead Heath in 1907. Howard envisaged a town "designed for health and industry", just large enough to constitute a social unit. His optimum number was round about 30,000 people, housed on 1,000 acres, with its large park, playground and public buildings, and around them a factory zone and a green belt surrounding the whole area. In 1903 First Garden City Ltd, was registered to build Letchworth in Hertfordshire for a population of 30,000 on a site of 3,800 acres, with a central area of 1,200 acres and an agricultural belt of 2,600 acres round it. Its post-war successor, Welwyn Garden City, was started in 1920.

The pioneers who founded these new communities set a standard and took the first steps towards making town planning into a specialised branch of knowledge. It was no longer enough for them that decent houses should be built. The stress now was on planning with an eye to future developments. The ideal community must have its residential area, and this must be so arranged as to secure maximum convenience, variety and beauty. Shopping areas and open spaces must be sufficient and sited within easy reach of dwellings; the industrial area must be set apart from the residential area, and roads must be planned and laid out to give the easiest access from one part to another, and also in and out of the whole community. Besides these, an infinite number of other precautions had to be taken to ensure that the ghastly mistakes of the early nineteenth century should not be repeated. In 1909 the work of these pioneers was recognised by the Government in the

"Designed for health and industry." Hampstead Garden
Suburb, opened in 1907

passing of the Housing and Town Planning Act which gave powers to local authorities to make and submit plans for building on parts of their districts which appeared most suitable, and then either to build on the plots themselves or allow building by private enterprise as long as it was in accordance with the approved plans.

Promising as these experiments were, few of the houses they produced were within reach of the wage-earner whose future depended either on what the local authority could do or what accommodation was provided by the speculative builder.

By 1900 every town council was alive to the problem. A publication compiled for the Health Committee of the Borough of Richmond, Surrey, states this very clearly.

"For many years the public have been aware of the grave evils arising from the inadequate and insanitary housing accommodation of the working classes in London and large towns, especially in industrial centres, but a remarkable phase of the question at present is the fact that an acute housing problem exists in nearly all the large villa districts near London, as well as in most fashionable watering places. . . . The evil is not confined to one section of the working classes. Many of these are steady, respectable people who are as much entitled to a clean, decent cottage at a moderate rent as the thriftless, intemperate and extremely indigent poor, whom many persons look on as the only section of the working classes that should be protected by the action of the municipality."

The booklet, in stating what should be done, divided the working classes into four groups, and states the type of housing appropriate to each one. The first, the "broken down", living precariously, could be catered for only by the provision of model lodging houses under supervision; the second, casual and irregularly employed, who were forced to live where they worked, in tenements of one or two rooms in crowded neighbourhoods; the third and fourth, regularly employed, earning 18s. to 30s. per week and 30s. to 40s. per week respectively, making up altogether 75 per cent. of the working-classes, in separate self-contained tenements or cottage houses, according to the neighbourhood, of from two to six rooms. The booklet goes on to list about a dozen local authorities in England and Wales which had already made a start by providing such dwellings.

One thing was clear. The one-room and two-room tenement in a crowded neighbourhood was not likely to solve the most pressing problem, that of congestion, and this fact was forcibly stated in a book published in the following year. The author of *Houses for the Working Classes in Urban Districts* (1900) contended that facilities for travel were good enough for a man to live some distance from his work and therefore it should be possible for him to live in a house. The book provided 30 typical and improved plans which private individuals or municipalities could adopt, and the author set out the requirements of the ideal dwelling for the wage-earner. The recommendations in this are interesting because one can compare them with the main features of the houses built round about that time which are still inhabited.

The most economical lay-out, says the author, was the terrace, because it meant less expenditure on outer walls, on fences and on the common sewer, which could be laid between the rows of back gardens. Economy in bricks could be achieved by application of concrete and rough-cast "which renders them (the houses) more weatherproof, and keeps the house both cooler in summer and warmer in winter." Bay windows, square or canted, were a necessity because they admitted the sun where otherwise it would not penetrate. The square bay could be coupled with the one belonging to the next house. A porch was desirable, paved with tiles, and leading into the entrance passage which should not be less than 2 ft. 9 in. wide, "enough space to accommodate a pram or a bicycle". This should be made as light as possible by means of a fanlight, and glazed door panels would be a help. The staircase should be lit from the entrance door and the landing window, and should be accessible without passing through a room. "Every advantage should be taken of the space under a staircase for storing coals etc." The living-room was meant to be both dining room and kitchen; the scullery floor should be paved and should have a sink and copper. Every house should have a bath if possible. This in smaller houses should be sunk into the scullery floor, supplied with cold water from the tap by the sink and with hot water from the copper. The W.C. should be entered from the backyard and should not be next to the pantry. "There is a general tendency to make the W.C. absurdly small. The minimum size should be 4 ft. 6 in. by 2 ft. 9 in."

These recommendations represent the best side of working-class housing at the turn of the century, and it was in dwellings of this kind though seldom even up to this standard that the suburban townsman made his home. The long rows of terrace houses spread out from the urban nuclei in what one writer calls "circles of incipient blight", swallowing up square miles of agricultural land, turning country lanes into town streets lined with houses and shops directly abutting on the narrow pavements. This development has left its mark on almost every modern town, so that one can see by a mere glance at a street map the twists and turns of the old lane, shut in on both sides by irregular rectangular systems of streets, gridiron-shaped, joined together by infilling, to make one vast, monotonous wilderness of brick. Much of the charm and individuality of building departed and though, through variation in colour and texture, brickwork could be made to look artistic it cost more money than the developer was prepared to lay out, and 1914 saw the expanding town encircled by this web of habitation. Many an interesting game could be played by collecting the names of these streets—Cawnpore, Magdala, Khartoum, Dongola, Buller, Lord Roberts and a thousand more, and actually dating the construction of the housing blocks.

In its expansion, the provincial city changed in shape and character. The mid-century had seen the whole complex—

houses, slums, offices and factories—crowded into one restricted space, the centre, and on one side was the fashionable quarter, a residential area of detached and semi-detached substantial houses belonging to the wealthier citizens. Then, as the city grew, throwing out arms along its lines of communication, other things happened. First around the centre grew a circle of closely packed working-class houses, many of them back-to-back. These were rapidly filled and eventually became the new slums, creeping out steadily and eventually standing cheek by jowl against the better class houses, often only separated from them by the breadth of a street, so that out of the front-room window one could see the whole length of the street opposite, with its long rows of windows and protruding doorsteps. Then, when communications, especially on the roads had improved and the railway station had been built, the better class resident moved right out of the town, either to a country house or even into the nearest seaside colony, leaving his old home either to be split off into tenements or rented as office premises, while the rash of terrace building crept gradually outwards.

The greatest volume of building was, as one would expect, around London. Stow, writing in 1603 of the road outside Aldgate, complains of the building of "filthy Cottages, and with other purprestures, inclosures and Laystalls . . . which is no small blemish to so famous a City, to have so unsavoury and unseemly an entry or passage thereunto". A similar sense of shame must certainly be felt by anybody who today has to begin his introduction of England to a foreign visitor with a view of suburban rooftops and cluttered backyards seen from a carriage window before entering one of London's main-line stations.

A very few talked and wrote about housing; a few more acted on their beliefs and created houses, but millions still remained, engulfed in the cities, the Great Wens of England, more extensive and stupendous growths than Cobbett ever dreamed of. They lived and still live, especially in London's environs, in long rows with serrated rooftops hidden from the street by the dirty yellow brick parapet, a relic of fashionable building in Georgian days. The overall plan is much the same everywhere—a 14-15 ft. frontage, the front door opening into the hall; a front room and back room downstairs and at the rear of the house an inner door leading into a kitchen-scullery which, paired with the one next door, sticks out into the two neighbouring small back gardens.

There are variations. Sometimes only front rooms have bays, sometimes both front and back, here and there you see bays carried up to the first floor. Sometimes, too, the kitchen-scullery projection is carried up to make a fourth bedroom. At first there were no bathrooms, only two bedrooms, front and back and a third over the hall, while the lavatory was in a little cabin joined to the main building with its door beyond the kitchen. But, as times changed, and especially as building societies were created and house ownership encouraged, one of the rooms upstairs was converted, with or without an upstairs lavatory, into a bathroom. Some of the houses, even the smaller ones, especially in East London and the boroughs beyond the Lea, had the tiniest front courtyards, extending not more than 3 ft. from the front door, but dignified by a gate and, before they were sawn off to make weapons of war, iron railings standing on a low wall. In the newer houses the roof, instead of being serrated with a long parapet, is one single long ridge roofed with the ubiquitous Welsh slate. This is a world of its own, crowded, friendly, cosy and untidy, especially on Sunday mornings when pavements are littered with Saturday night's fried fish papers and castaway race track programmes. But even here beauty has a place where self-respecting borough councils have put through sound road-widening programmes and erected handsome public buildings, while on a smaller scale some of the tiny back gardens in summer time burst forth into a riot of colour.

The invasion of the countryside by urban development which gained momentum between 1850 and 1914 was only made possible by the establishment and growth of public services. The city business man would not have been able to travel his twenty or thirty miles a day to work without the railway. Even the clerk and the skilled artisan could afford to move out a distance of three or even four miles and travel to work by the street tram, drawn first by horses and then, after about 1900, electrically driven. The electric tramcar was indeed a marvel when it first appeared and its first trip on the streets was celebrated with illuminations in many a city.

Water and gas services, often started by private companies and then in some cases taken over by local authorities, provided the water and the light which made for cleaner, pleasanter houses and tidier, well-lit streets. Even these improvements were not brought about without some protests, for they could not be introduced without raising the rates. Many a householder, hoping to avoid these higher payments, moved out of the town into newly-developed estates in the adjacent countryside only to find in a few years that he was overtaken by the new conditions and compelled to pay both higher rates and higher fares to town. There are examples, especially, around London, of the inhabitants of whole housing estates protesting against the making up and lighting of their streets.

At the same time that public services expanded, industry was providing an increasing supply of goods designed to improve the comfort of domestic life. Some of these were new, some had been in existence a long time, but had only been in use among the wealthy. Well into the twentieth century the outdoor earth closet, emptied periodically, was almost universal in working-class homes, though in some schools the "tippler" system was installed with a sort of underground reservoir serving a series of cubicles and emptying into the sewage. The valve closet was invented as early as 1596 by Sir John Harrington, but water closets of any kind were not generally installed in any but the larger houses until just before the 1914-18 war, again not without complaints of these "newfangled contraptions" which wasted water and put up the rates. Some houses had built-in baths before the installation of back boilers, but most had to wait until the occupant could enjoy the luxury of a hot-water tap.

Gas, which came into use for street lighting at the beginning of the nineteenth century, did not reach the home until about 1870. At first the union jet or fishtail burner was used because it spread the flame, on the edges of which carbon particles burnt a bright yellow, giving a steady but rather faint light. The Welsbach mantle, the fruit of a half-century of experiment into the luminosity of various materials suspended in the gas flame, was patented in 1886, bringing the possibility of good clear yellow light within the reach of all. The brass chandelier with its two or three brilliant cones of light seen through flower-like globes of glass, was a common feature of the "best room". The used gas mantle, white and flimsy, would fall to dust at the slightest touch, and when the light had to be cleaned it needed the steadiest hand to take off the globe, remove the mantle from its white porcelain fork with a small knitting needle and suspend it in space until it could be replaced with equal care after the jet had been blown out.

The modern treatment of floors did not come until after 1800. Bare boards were common, though because they let in the draughts they were often partially covered by some kind of home-made rug or carpet. Stone and brick floors were often sanded. The invention of oil cloth and later of linoleum helped to brighten up a living-room, and give an air of comfort, though on a stone floor it wore unevenly, and the harbouring of damp under it brought smells and encouraged the breeding of vermin. Wallpaper was not much used in the working-class home until after 1861 when the Paper Tax was repealed. By that time the cylinder printing machine had brought prices within reach and turned the once whitewashed wall into a veritable indoor garden.

With all these improvements, life was still simple and the woman's work was, in truth, never done, for the week, with

Monday's washing, Thursday's baking and Friday's cleaning for the weekend with all the shopping, cooking, sweeping, mending and bedmaking in between times, was a continual round of labour. Washing for a household with dolly, rubbing-board and roller-mangle, taxed the endurance of the strongest. In crowded districts hanging-space was insufficient and garments were often spotted with soot before they were brought in. Even men's outer garments had to be carefully washed to prevent shrinking, for there was no dry cleaning. Charcoal irons and flat-irons heated on gas rings made for tedium and backache. The Friday housework, when the range and oven were literally cleaned with "spit and polish", the black lead breathed on and brushed till it shone like coal, when the floors were washed all over with soap and floorcloth, was both hard on the knees and exhausting. On that day everything had to be made spick and span for Saturday and Sunday when the family were at home. Shopping, when there was little tinned or dried or packeted food and no refrigeration, had to be done more often and there was greater bulk to carry home. Given good health the task was not impossible. Many a married couple succeeded in feeding, housing, clothing and giving good education to their children on £2 a week. Clean windows with plants, flagstones scrubbed buff and gold, doorsteps shining with yellowstone and ridged with white redeemed many a street from sordidness. In days when horse traffic, except for the milk float or greengrocer's cart, rarely entered it could be neighbourly and safe, even for children.

X

The Face of the Land

Fifty years of publicity, planning and legislation had made both national and local government conscious of the great need for clearing slum areas and providing sufficient good houses for the growing population, but it had done little more. Though the spread of slums had been largely checked, clearance had barely begun and the amount of housing provided by local authorities and societies was no more than about 5 per cent. of the whole. Owing to rising costs the production of houses, even by private enterprise, had fallen off, so that by the outbreak of war in 1914 there was great scarcity of accommodation. By 1918 the situation was immeasurably worse. The birth rate had gone up owing to the large number of war marriages, and the sudden re-entry into civilian life of what was left of the nation's young manhood brought about a sudden and acute demand. House-hunting became a regular pastime and was the subject of many a music-hall joke. To the young couple with children who had to share the accommodation of their parents and in-laws it was a much more serious matter.

The man who came back from the war had expected to find both a job and a house to live in. With regard to the latter, the Government with its slogan "Homes for Heroes" had encouraged him in this expectation. Nevertheless, it was beyond the powers of any government to supply the half million or more houses that were urgently needed. The most that could be done was to lay on the local authorities the statutory obligation to build and to encourage the private builder and the housing society by making grants. This was done in the Housing Act of 1919, when the Government took responsibility for the payment of any sum which exceeded that raised by 1d. rate on any approved housing scheme. Private builders were granted subsidies which averaged about £240 a house, and housing societies were helped by the payment of a proportion of their interest and redemption charges. By this system of subsidy, which was carried on almost without a break after 1919, the Government recognised that housing was no longer a problem which concerned only the private builder, the benevolent employer or the housing society, but one which had to be dealt with on a nation-wide basis. Thus its scope widened to include regional planning and the building of the satellite towns.

Slum clearance was part of the same question and was the subject of a series of acts culminating in that of 1930, which called on local authorities to submit their plans for the next five years and which granted a subsidy for every person re-housed. No single act was a complete success, but partly as a result of government action, and partly as a result of the gradual recovery after the grave financial crisis of 1931, the building process gathered momentum, and between 1935 and 1939 the number of family units in houses and apartments rose to some 75,000 a year built by the local authorities and 350,000 a year built by private enterprise. The construction of new dwellings, however, proceeded much more swiftly than the clearance of slums, and for a generation Britain presented a more striking contrast than ever, not this time between the small rich minority and the great mass of the poor, but between the comfortable suburban families living mainly in the south and east, and those in the north, in Lancashire, in the West Riding and Northumberland living on unemployment pay in the mean streets of towns where the factory chimneys had ceased to smoke and the shipyards were closed for lack of orders.

The years between the wars, therefore, saw another stage in the expansion of the provincial town, the gradual appearance of blots of pink roofs on its periphery, swallowing up

Semi-detached houses of the inter-war years, showing ribbon development along a two-track road. Spring Grove, Great West Road, 1931

large stretches of countryside, leaving only here and there an irregular green shape reserved for park or recreation ground. The new buildings had a special tendency to cling closely to the main roads leading to and from the centre of the city, often stretching out miles into the countryside; long terrace rows, each house with its front garden; or blocks of "semis" drawn closely together with not much more room between them than would allow for a couple of side doors leading into the back gardens. The front-garden gates opened directly on to the kerb, and in many cases there was not even a grass verge to separate it from the road. For the first time the phrase "ribbon development" came into common use, and though from the beginning this kind of planning was condemned it went on, especially around London and the larger towns. Most ribbon development was the work of the private builder.

In other places, town councils taking advantage of Government help, erected council houses, sometimes in small detached units, sometimes in larger settlements or whole communities. Each council drew up its housing list, placing applicants in order of preference on a points system or, if the new estate was combined with a slum clearance plan, re-housing whole neighbourhoods in new and strange surroundings.

The up-and-coming middle-class tended to look with disdain on both the council house and its tenants in the days between the wars. Some of the early attempts of the public authorities, though they provided all the amenities required for approval such as hot and cold water, bath and indoor W.C., were sadly lacking in taste. Though the streets were generally open and wide, letting in the sun and air, the view of rows of small houses unrelieved by bays or porches had a rather grim look, especially when the smoke discoloured the bricks and turned roughcast frontages to a dingy grey. There were dismal prophecies as to what would happen to these neighbourhoods after a few years, that they would be turned into the the new twentieth-century slums, and stories were told of tenants who used the bath as a coal store and took neighbours' fences for firewood. The council house created a new social class which took some years to become absorbed. Slum clearance especially came in for its share of abuse, particularly from the residents of neighbourhoods near to where the migrants were to be settled because, they said, the proximity of a housing estate of this type lowered the value of their homes.

Where people were to be accommodated in their thousands in one single settlement there were more things to think about than the mere erection of houses, and some idea of the problems to be faced may be gathered from the creation and development of the Borough of Dagenham. Here on the open land between Barking and Hornchurch the London County Council was given legal sanction to purchase land for the housing of some of its overcrowded population. The new

Becontree Estate was completed as far as building was concerned within about ten years of the commencement of work in 1922, but there were difficulties from the beginning. First, before the new Dagenham Urban District was created in 1926 the area to be developed lay within the boundaries of three local authorities, one a borough, the second an urban district and the third a parish, all under the Essex County Council but within the Metropolitan police area, while other bodies controlled the supply of water, gas and electricity. Secondly the constant changing of the amounts and the basis of government grants caused uneven and often sporadic progress.

The conception of a new self-governing town was bold, and the physical planning of the huge estate was good, but there was much in the beginning that was lacking, for besides houses people need good roads, easy travelling facilities, satisfactory sewage disposal, refuse collection, public open spaces, street lighting, hospitals, public health services, libraries and adequate provision for education. "I doubt," says the Dagenham historian, "if the original promoters of the scheme realised its vast implications and the endless ripples that this stone would create, which they threw into the quiet pool of Dagenham." It was not until the Urban District was finally created with its own self-governing council that the ancillary services were able to catch up with the rapid pace at which the building of houses progressed.

By that time the value of a new Thames-side location had been realised by industry. The establishment and growth of the Ford Motor Works and other industrial concerns brought an influx of population and an even more urgent demand for community services. By prodigious efforts the Council and officers of the new authority managed to make up lost ground with the result that in 1938 Dagenham received its charter as a borough and had services which would bear comparison with any in the outer metropolitan area. The lesson of Dagenham, which bore fruit in the construction of the post-war satellite town, was that it must be conceived and planned from the beginning as a community, that provision for educational, social and cultural services must go hand in hand with that of housing, growing with functions balanced so that within it the individual might have the opportunity of living a full and complete life. The Dagenham venture had proved once again that in the twentieth century, as in all other ages, the home could not be considered apart from the community in which it stood.

The 1919 Act was the first which included provisions for helping private builders, and with the aid of housing subsidies they did much to ease the situation, though in general they catered for the professional classes and the better-off workers. As the 'thirties approached, the building boom gathered momentum, reaching its climax in the two years before the outbreak of the second World War. During this period the buying of new houses was encouraged by the building societies which in general were willing to lend on them a greater proportion of the total cost than they were on older houses. Young couples in particular found this a great help in home-building and flocked into the new estates.

Excluding the superior detached house, the type of two-storey dwelling differed little in broad plan from the pre-war terrace house. The favourite type was the semi-detached villa with a front garden and side entrance door leading to another garden at the back. If the side entrance was wide enough it might be occupied by a coal store, though later, when more families acquired motor cars, the coal shed disappeared to make room for a garage.

The hall of the semi-detached house was usually wider than that of the terrace house, and was sufficient to accommodate a staircase and a door into the kitchen so that one need not pass through the living room at the back to get into it. There were the usual front and back downstairs rooms, the front one with a semi-circular bay or less frequently a square one, sometimes continued up to the best bedroom, and the back room on the ground floor often having a french window leading into the

garden. These houses differed from some pre-war ones, especially in the north in that they had neither cellars nor attics.
The loft, often used as storage space, was accessible through a
square trap let into a ceiling. The lack of cellar space had its
drawbacks and before refrigerators became common many a
family had to resort to such measures as storing food and milk
in biscuit tins or other containers buried in a shady spot near
the house.

No architect was needed to plan such houses as these. With
little variation they appeared in their thousands, brick-built
except in stone-bearing areas where the lower storey might be
of stone, or at least stone-faced, and roofed with plain pink
tiles, occasionally with pantiles or with Welsh slate if it was
accessible and cheap. Upper storeys and sometimes whole
frontages were faced with roughcast. This took away the raw
look from the expanses of brick and tile, but caused many a
doubt in the mind of the old-fashioned householder as to what
kind of workmanship was hidden underneath the shell. Vague
assertions about jerry-building were bandied around, and the
utmost scorn was poured on the new-fangled breeze blocks
coming into general use for the partition walls. The new
building methods came in handy as a stock joke for the
comedian of the day:

> If you should sneeze in one house and the next one
> tumbles down
> It will all come out of the rates,

sang Fred Duprez. Gracie Fields dwelt more on the snob
approach:

> Our Avenue is a nice Avenue
> Have-a-new house down our Avenue,

or "We're all living at the Cloisters", in a select area which, if
the occupant could not pay his rent, was "cloise-to the workhouse." Pride in ownership demanded that a house should
have a name. Young couples commemorated their honey-
moon by Lugano or Alassio, Bella Vista, Sans Souci, Chez
Nous and Mon Abri; on a lower level were such names as

Dunromin, Adenuff, Billanive and Mumzome. Affluence was on the way, though a war had to be waged before it became a way of life.

As the number of houses increased, the limited nomenclature of Street, Lane and Road was no longer sufficient. Terrace and Avenue appeared before the beginning of the present century and were followed by such names as Walk, Way, Crescent and Drive. There were Chases where nobody followed the hounds, unenclosed Closes, Views without scenery and Groves without trees.

Single-storey habitations, in existence from time immemorial, continued throughout the centuries, mainly for the humblest labouring families. In the late nineteenth century, another one-storey house appeared. This was the bungalow. The word, deriving from the Hindustani (*bangla*–belonging to Bengal) was first applied to the type of dwelling lived in by Europeans in India. In its original form it had an overhanging roof and a verandah. It became common in England as a country or seaside residence. Then, when the advantages of the one-storey dwelling became apparent, bungalows were built in large numbers, principally on the outskirts of towns. Since they needed more land than the two-storey houses and

Bungalows, detached and semi-detached. Benfleet, Essex, 1938-9

For those who could afford it the individually-planned detached bungalow offered the opportunity for distinctive designs. A house at Buckhurst Hill, Essex

were detached, the cost per cubic foot of living space was higher, and therefore they were almost invariably put up by the private builder.

In the English type, the projecting roof, except when it overhangs a bay, has almost disappeared, and few bungalows have verandahs. Once the single-storey house had become established as a type, almost any one, whatever its size or shape, went by the name of bungalow. Town dwellers, especially in East London, bought plots of land farther out in Essex and there erected shacks of wood and plaster with a minimum of convenience, and these too they called bungalows. In the 'thirties, builders were laying out whole estates in which semi-detached bungalows appeared. In the end, the word, especially coined to distinguish this new type from the common cottage, came to be applied to any building of one storey, while the word "cottage" tended to do the opposite. Thus the poor man, hard put to it to pay his monthly mortgage money might live in a bungalow, while the rich company director spent his leisure hours at his luxurious country cottage, complete with tennis court and swimming pool. Now the two terms are so widely applied that they are almost interchangeable. Even the bungalow, once a single-storey building, may, by the addition of rooms in the roof space, become a chalet bungalow.

The great changes which took place inside the English home between the wars worked mainly in two directions: to increase the comfort of home life, and to decrease the drudgery of housework. There were few households which did not possess a carpet, and the old-fashioned home-made rug became a thing of the past. Where the carpet did not cover the whole floor there was inlaid lino which did not lose its pattern through wear and was easy to wipe over. The taste grew for heavier and springier upholstery, and the smallest sitting room, now coming to be called the lounge, might contain a three-piece suite big enough to sink into but hard to move around on cleaning days. Hire purchase, especially of furniture, became widespread, and firms opened up which specialised in this trade, saving the customer's face by delivery in plain vans.

The fire, for centuries the nucleus of the home, was beginning to lose part of its functions. It still provided hot water, though the old-fashioned range was fast disappearing and the side-pan had given way to the back boiler with pipes connecting it to the kitchen sink and the bathroom. In the heating field its earliest rival was gas, which up to about 1920 had almost monopolised the interior lighting of houses and was already gaining ground as a warming agent since the invention of the brightly-glowing radiant. Cooking by gas was at first done on rings and simple gas ovens, but the combination grill, ring and cooker was fast coming into use. Electricity arrived a little later, first in competition in lighting, and then in heating and power. The great lighting duel lasted well into the 'thirties and ended in a complete victory for electricity. The competition in cookers, and to a smaller extent in refrigerators, continued.

The great advantage of electricity was as a source of power.

At first, irons and vacuum cleaners appeared with names such as Hoover and Electrolux. Sewing machine firms began to produce power models and these became common early in the thirties. Refrigerators and washing machines were not frequently seen even in the lower middle-class home before the Second World War, though they were beginning to be installed in new properties as early as about 1935, and were rapidly improving in design and adaptability. These varied appliances brought ease to the housewife and a complete revolution in housekeeping, assisted by such outside agencies as the dry-cleaner's shop. The labour of preparing and cooking food was lessened by the increasing supply and variety of tinned and powdered goods. Popular interest in good house-keeping and familiarity with methods, appliances and materials was considerably increased by the rapid growth in circulation of magazines which catered specially for the home-maker, first the wife whose concern was with beauty and efficiency and later the handyman husband.

At the same time a great change came over home entertainment. Up to the 'twenties the piano remained supreme, and might be heard almost any evening or Sunday morning as one walked along any street, but its days were numbered. When in 1876 Thomas Alva Edison succeeded in reproducing sounds by recording their vibrations on a moving surface, nobody realised what enormous changes in social behaviour his discovery would bring about. The first machines, with their wax cylinders and great horns like giant convolvuli, were followed by cabinet gramophones with discs or plate records and the internal speaker. Then, shortly after the First World War, came the wireless, first the crystal set worked by tickling the crystal with the "cat's whisker" and listening through earphones, then the valve set with loud-speaker horn. For years gramophone and radio remained separate until in the late 'thirties the radio-gramophone appeared. This was the pointer to a new age of entertainment. No longer did one hear the pianos, but the blare of the radio penetrated everywhere, and was often a nuisance in summer when windows were left open. Pianoforte and music teachers declined in numbers as the demand for lessons fell off. The transition to mechanical means of home entertainment and entertainment in general was well under way when war broke out in 1939.

The repeal in 1896 of the act which made it compulsory to have a red flag carried in front of mechanically-propelled vehicles, brought on to the roads of England a new phenomenon. Harry Tate celebrated its noise and unreliability in his sketch "Motoring". London buses were used to transport troops to the front line at the beginning of the First World War and though fun was poked at the would-be motorist in popular songs the motor-car had come to stay, and with it came another change which affected English home life. The suburbanite in his semi, having paid off a good part of his mortgage, began to prepare for the next great advance in standard of living, setting apart one side of his garden and laying down a concrete run-in against the day when he would have another mechanical addition to his family. The pattern of middle-class life was evolving.

In the 1930s the face of England must have been as ugly and depressing as at any period in modern times. Poverty in the depressed areas, especially in the north of the country, remained, and slum clearance had removed as yet only a small percentage of the black spots in the towns. But poverty and distress was not the only cause. Another was the half-blind approach in other parts of the country towards a more affluent way of living. The new housing estates lay like great red sores on the countryside, old villages were scarred by their picturesque cottages being overlooked or quite surrounded by rows of harsh vulgar-looking red-brick houses. "Bungaloid growths", as they were often scornfully called, were dotted here and there on the open countryside, their streets as yet unmade, and with no approach to them save by way of deeply-rutted bridle paths which became quagmires in wet weather. New patterns of settlement turned ancient country lanes into important highways too narrow as yet to carry the traffic which crowded on to them.

The sale in lots of cheap land within reach of large towns encouraged the proliferation of temporary shacks and huts built with few conveniences for rough-and-ready weekends and holidays. In such places the once clean countryside became a rural slum, streams turned foul by the deposits of refuse, old paper, empty tin cans, bicycle wheels and rusty bedsteads. More and more advertisements for such commodities as pills, petrol, distemper and newspapers offended the eye at every turn of the road and in every village. These, "the countryside's everlasting flowers", disfigured trees, defiled the sides of barns and the green hedges.

As road traffic increased, so did the haphazard developments along the highways, especially on the approaches to towns, where a mixture of repair shops, scattered light industry, petrol stations, new housing and pull-in cafés lined the road in no order or plan. But it was not this alone which gave cause for concern. In terms of building the Englishman began to ask himself, "Where is all this to end?" and he saw little beyond further degradation and confusion. The only redeeming features were the model housing schemes set up by public authorities such as that of the L.C.C. at Edgware, or by industry as at Billingham (I.C.I.) and at Silver End, Essex, by Crittalls, and the still small voice of such institutions as the Design and Industries Association and the Council for the Preservation of Rural England. On a deeper level, writers and poets were bemoaning the social effects of all these changes. D. H. Lawrence deplored the rush for possessions and the rise of the "beastly bourgeois". Priestley, Orwell and Greenwood saw with unease the widening division of the country into haves and have-nots, into north and south. In 1939 all speculation was ended by the outbreak of the Second World War.

XI

New Trends

After 1945 housing was the most pressing question of the day, at least in the realm of home affairs. The situation was worse, if anything, than it had been in 1918, for this time the enemy bomber had laid waste the centres of many English towns and reduced them to craggy wildernesses overgrown with grass, wild flowers and young saplings. Some idea of the destruction may be gathered from the figures for one borough alone— West Ham, where out of 50,800 buildings over 14,000 had been demolished or so badly damaged that they had to be taken down. Of these by far the greater number were houses. There was, however, one consolation. The damage done by the German bombers gave the local authorities the chance to purchase sites and to put on them better dwellings than had been there before.

The machinery was already there and was made more effective by the Acts of 1946 and 1949. The Government was fully involved, and the authorities had power to act. But at first progress was slow. Skilled labour was hard to find, and materials, especially bricks and timber, were in short supply. When, immediately after the war, the rebuilding of a house had been sanctioned, it could take anything up to a year or fifteen months for it to be completed.

In the public sector the emphasis was on community development, and the lessons learnt as a result of early experiments were applied in the creation of the new satellite towns. Construction was preceded by a period of detailed planning, with time-scheme as well as lay-out, and as the work progressed it included the balancing of every aspect of home and community life. Besides the judicious siting of baths, health centres and community halls, there are many other features of the modern new town that immediately strike the eye.

The most important is the amount of open space and its balance with the built-up areas. Housing stands well back from the main roads, and even in minor ones there is evidence of the effort to gain for every dwelling an open vista, grid-iron formations of long monotonous streets being avoided by irregular planning and varying distances from the road. Industry is located in its own special zones, in premises which are not, as the old nineteenth-century factories were, an offence to the eye.

Of housing there is a variety of type, one of the most interesting features being the retention of the terrace house which makes for both cheapness and economy in the use of land. The new examples of this type are grouped so as to avoid monotony and though constructed on similar plans, are varied by the use of different materials, minor features and colours, and are not unpleasing. The common frontage of many of them, opening on to greens, adds to the attractiveness. In the mid-fifties the planners also recognised that the working man might also be able to purchase his own private means of transport, and almost every group of terrace houses is accompanied by its row of courtyard garages.

A return has also been made to the medieval conception of a street as a place where people may walk, meet, talk and make purchases, and so the main shopping precinct at least is separated from the highway, and when it is in two or three parts these are connected by pedestrian ways, the kind of alley from which at one time wheeled traffic had to be excluded by the erection of posts. Thus, with its lightness, its airiness and its many novel features, the atmosphere of the new town is quite different from that of the nineteenth century, and is so much more attractive that the councils of older towns are replanning and reserving certain streets in their own town centres for pedestrian shoppers.

Unlike the French or the Scots, the English have not as a

nation taken kindly to living in flats. Poverty and the need to crowd many people into limited space brought about the construction of tenement houses in the Middle Ages, and Stow tells us that after the monasteries were dissolved much of the land left vacant was filled with small tenements let out at high rents to "meane people", and the same thing happened to the houses left by wealthier inhabitants who sought pleasanter sites on Thames-side near Westminster. The pressure of population and the high price of houses early in the present century also tempted householders near London and in other towns, especially in the south, to let off one floor to another family, both families using the same entrance, with use of the bathroom by the ground-floor tenants about once a week by arrangement, and sometimes with both families using the same kitchen. This lack of self-containment often led to disagreements, clashes of temperament and a great deal of unhappiness. The ideal part-accommodation was the self-contained flat and many of these were built between the wars.

The demolition of bombed areas and the need for slum clearance confronted public authorities with the problem on a larger scale. How was it possible to house a large number of people on a small area and at the same time to provide open spaces and facilities for community life? The answer was to build upwards, and the result has been the erection of hundreds of skyscraper blocks. The flat has now become a prominent feature of the English town scene. The lessons drawn from one experiment in this kind of building had to be applied to the next. Where there was room, the ideal was a mixed unit. Architecturally the mingling of tower blocks with lower-, four- or five-storey maisonnettes, the altitude gradually shading off to harmonize with the adjacent streets of two-storey houses, made for a varied scene and a less rugged skyline.

Another aspect of mixed development was the bringing together of people of all ages and of more than one social class. It was recognised, for instance, that it was not good for old people who were as much members of a community as others, to be segregated in separate areas, and provision was made for them as well as for single persons and married couples with children. Social class did not enter as much into the question, for since there was little unemployment and wages were better for the workers than they had ever been, the material difference between them and the so-called lower middle-class had disappeared. The plans of such units varied considerably with regard to the shape and arrangement of the blocks. Some were disposed around a circle, ellipse or rectangle, enclosing the open space, a large common garden with trees and paths. Others were composed of blocks irregularly placed and with short terrace rows, straight or gently curving, disposed between them so that all had advantages of sunshine at some time

Scyscraper flats, London Borough of Newham

of the day and access to open spaces. Some blocks were cruci-form, some Y-shaped, so that all the wings could be served by one central stair and lift.

At first the building of tower blocks seemed to offer an ideal solution to the problem of high density housing in spite of the fact that they are 50 per cent more expensive per person housed than in the ordinary dwelling, but fifteen years of experience have revealed many unforeseen drawbacks. Some of these are physical. The weather is worse the higher one goes and more insulation is needed. Even the air can be polluted on still days in autumn or winter when the products of combus-tion from the stoves in houses below, gather on the top of a blanket of mist or fog. Other difficulties arise from fear; the fear of heights, the feeling that nothing but a sheet of glass separates one from the infinity of sky and space outside; the fear of disasters such as the one at Ronan Point in 1968 when a gas explosion caused the collapse of one side of a block, the fear of fire or being trapped in a broken-down lift.

High living has proved especially difficult for mothers with young children. The landings cannot be used as playgrounds and neighbours object to noise. Proximity can be a bar and not a help to neighbourliness, especially when doors and windows all face outwards and nobody lives opposite. Stairs, and land-ings except those immediately adjoining, are foreign territory where many of the people one meets are strangers. Suspicion runs high, and some of the doors, fitted with spy-holes and chains, are cautiously opened when one knocks. For some, the fresh air, the light, the warmth and modern living is hardly a compensation for life at ground level. For many the preference is still for a house with a front and back garden. Those who come off best are the persons and small families that are more self-sufficient, those who can close the doors and pull the curtains in the evening and with the television or the quiet home pursuit, shut out the world. For others, a process of adaptation is required, together with increased provisions on the part of the authorities to foster community life.

Lucky is the man who can guide his own motor-mower over his own lawn, who can drill holes with impunity into the interior walls of his own property, who can wallow in peat and bone meal and work off his aggressive instincts on green-fly and thrip in his own garden. All other social questions aside, he is secure and from this haven of his he may put out his efforts in any direction he pleases. Free to conform, free to be selfish or philanthropic, free to serve many causes or none, he is lord of his castle, unassailable by any adversity save the major ones such as loss of health or unemployment. He too may now play a major rôle in the domestic drama, for the do-it-yourself drive has made him an active participant. He may be his own home-builder, decorator, carpenter, plumber, window-cleaner and sweep, especially if he lives in a bunga-low where he has no need to risk the safety of his limbs with extension ladders.

A wide variety of industries has arisen to satisfy his needs. Paints with gloss, eggshell, plain and emulsion finishes exist in variety, curtains slide almost inaudibly on the latest plastic fitting. He may parquet his own floors or cover them with stick-on tiles, double-glaze his windows with framed plastic, insulate his roof with glass fibre or vermiculite and his walls and ceiling with polystyrene. His toolbox abounds with mechanical gadgets which bore, saw, buff and sand. Gas and electricity, oil and solid fuel compete for his custom in the heating field, and even his central heating may be bought in a do-it-yourself kit. Everything is made easy with sheets of instructions complete to the fixing of the last joint, and the home-maker's magazine which drops weekly through his letter-box supplies him with all the latest ideas and information.

In the general all-out drive to get rid of drudgery, nobody has benefited more than the housewife. The magic of abrasives and detergents is ready at hand. Stains are removed from garments by chemical agents and the minute organisms called enzymes which literally eat the stains off. Washing machines, spin dryers, drying cabinets have done away with the need for outdoor clothes lines, and drip-dry fabrics have lessened the quantity of garments to be ironed. Vacuum cleaners have been perfected and electric power has been adapted for use in the mixing of cakes, the drying of hair, the heating of water and home vibratory massage. The pre-packing of food has abolished the need for elaborate preparation of meals apart from table-laying. Automatic dishwashers and waste removal units take over the disagreeable tasks after the meal is over. Such appliances are used in varying degrees according to one's inclinations and resources. But though all these exist, there are some housewives who have to stick to most of the old time-honoured methods of housekeeping, and others who prefer to do so.

The social effects of this revolution have become apparent in the last twenty years, for the home of today is more than ever a place to abide in, especially in the winter. Our grandfathers and our fathers' generation sallied out of doors on an evening to the penny reading, the ballad concert, the public house and the cinema. We go along a street on an evening and see the blue glow of the television screen in one house after another. Where, not much more than a generation ago, the streets were alive with footfalls, to-day little is seen on an evening except near pubs, youth clubs and bingo halls beyond the odd pedestrian and the continuous moving headlights of cars.

Deeper social effects, the loneliness of the old, the malaise of the middle-aged and the discontent of the young are beyond the scope of this work, but one group, those who have been left behind in the struggle for the decent home, cannot be forgotten.

The existence of this group arises from two main causes, the high cost of house purchase and the expense of travelling to work. House prices since 1945 have risen out of all proportion to the cost of living. Terrace houses which cost £400 are now £3,000, semi-detached three-bedroomed houses selling at £1,000 have gone up to the same figure; pre-war bungalows erected in 1938 for £450 fetch anything up to ten times the price. New properties are just as expensive. Money is dear, and even though a person may be willing to buy a house he has to satisfy the society lending the money that he is in employment which will give a reasonable guarantee that he will be able to pay his monthly instalments. For a person with little or no reserve cash, house-buying is impossible; there are few houses to be rented from private owners at a reasonable figure and to obtain a council house or flat one has to wait one's turn on a points list. Tenants of long standing are fortunate because they enjoy a certain amount of protection. It is the newcomer and the newly married couple without a bank balance who are most exposed to the hazards of homelessness and exploitation.

The exposure of such hazards as these by the Rachman case and in the television play "Cathy come Home" revealed the shocking state of affairs in some parts of the overcrowded cities of Britain. Here in streets of old but once respectable houses live families, each occupying one or two rooms. The houses, mostly owned by absentee landlords, are falling to ruin through lack of repair. Walls are damp and cannot be decorated, there is no sufficient water-supply, no washing facilities, electric wiring is rotten and unusable and many families have no source of heat save an oil stove. The toilet, often on another floor, has to be used by two or three families and is in a disgraceful condition and the premises are overrun by rats and mice. Appeals to the local councils are of little avail, overburdened as these authorities are with whole streets of properties whose occupants all need rehousing. Societies such as "Shelter" have been formed to make the plight of such families and to attempt to relieve at least those worst affected.

For those who can afford it the speculative builder has much to offer, and the second half of the present century has seen many breaks with tradition. The familiar "semi" of the inter-war years has almost completely disappeared from the new building plans which offer far greater variation. The modern estate developer, having acquired the land, plans the number, size and siting of the houses that are to be placed on it having regard to various considerations such as the aspect, direction and degree of slope, the means of access to the nearest town, and the type of buyer that his estate is likely to attract. Then, every estate of any size contains several types of houses, often given brand names, and these can be fitted with extra features to suit the needs of the buyer. The garden wall, so prominent a feature in the early years of the century, is tending to disappear and the front doors often open on to an expanse of grass and flowers with paths and drives running across it. Almost every house has its garage, either built into the main building, projecting from one wing, or completely detached. Porches, once a familiar feature, have almost disappeared, giving place to a simple projection which serves as a shelter over the front door. Where porches do exist, they have lost their old ornamental character and appear as simple cubes, flat-roofed with glass sides. Glass doors and windows are a prominent feature of the new type of house and sometimes may extend along the whole length of one side, with a large pane in the centre for which we have invented the term "picture-window". The detached house, the semi, the chalet, the bungalow and the terrace house all appear in various guises. Roofs, even of the detached and semi-detached houses are low-pitched, carrying little weight, while those of chalets are much steeper, with either dormer or half-dormer windows rising from the roofs. New building materials make it possible for a house to have a completely watertight flat roof, making the use of tiles unnecessary. Where roofs slope, however, tiles, including pantiles, appear in an extraordinary variety of shapes and colours. The tile-hanging of walls, once common only in the southeast, especially Kent and Sussex, may now be seen in any part of the country: Stone-faced buildings are still common in the north, and imitation coursed or uncoursed rubble facings can be bought and laid either on to bricks, plaster or wood as facing. Weatherboard, once commonly used only in the

Modern terrace houses, with tiled roof, tile-hung upper storey, cedar cladding and open frontage

south-east, has been adopted in many new buildings, especially between upstairs windows, and is generally painted white. When the brickwork is showing it is usually laid in stretching bond, that is, with no headers, but line after line of stretchers. In larger buildings, to add a little more firmness to a wall, a line of headers is to be found between four or five lines of stretchers.

The interior of the modern house has the same specialised rooms as before, the living-room, dining-room and kitchen. In the fifties the open-plan house found great favour, with living-dining-rooms as one unit, the dining space being near to one of the windows, while the kitchen was separated from it only by a waist-high dividing wall used for resting dishes, or passing them from one room to another. The most extreme open plan included an open stair to the bedroom above. Later this one-unit downstairs room tended to lose favour owing to the fact that when occupied by a family it did not give enough privacy to the various members. There are still, however, kitchen-dining rooms and dining-living rooms while the open stair leading from one or the other is far more economical of space than the closed-in staircase, and has the advantage of not needing stair carpet. All this is made the more feasible by the most-publicised innovation of all in England–central heating. Some large units are now centrally heated by a single installation, thus saving expense. The Englishman has long been a devotee of the open fire:

A good roarin' fire and the kettle on the boil,
It makes a fellow happy when he's done his daily toil;
A tidy wee wifie and a clean hearthstone–
Oh it's very very cosy when a fellow comes home.

But those days are passing as the younger generation becomes accustomed to a uniform temperature diffused day and night through the whole house.

Prefabrication, a method of house-building employed for single units in the days of half-timber, has returned with the increasing use of concrete and plastics as building materials, but in modern days pre-fabrication implies mass-production. By this means it is possible to erect a house with all its fittings on a prepared site in a very short space of time, but the number of prefabricated houses produced still falls far short of the number produced by straightforward building methods. In any case, with land prices as they are and with a large proportion of the cost of a house going into ancillary services such as the making up of roads, the laying below surface at increasingly deeper levels of telephone cables, electricity, gas mains, water mains, drains and sewers and the connection of these to the house, the price of the completed building cannot be greatly reduced even by prefabrication. Membership of the property-owning democracy is still out of reach of a large section of the population.

In the realms of home-making at least, money talks. For those who can produce it there are still more variations such as the Scandinavian or Swiss designs with dormers, outshuts, double garages, upstairs and downstairs bathrooms and spacious entrance halls, or continental models with semi-basements containing garage, cellar fuel store and central heating installation, and over it the *"piano rialzato"* or raised ground floor with a wide flight of steps to the front door and low terrace with French windows. Staircases lead to the first floor which also has its long terrace and into the roof space, used for storage. On top of all this may be a roof garden.

We pass from this to the dream-city of the future. Exhibited at the Montreal World's Fair was the sensational twelve-storey development called Habitat 67, designed by a Canadian architect. This was not a block of flats, but a pile of single, fully-detached family houses, arranged in storeys, and one on the other in such a way that every house has its garden and its own front door leading on to a "street" with no contact between the ceilings, floors or walls of adjacent houses. There are 60-ft. wide roads on two levels of the building and children's playgrounds in the sky.

Another thought-provoking design appeared at the same time—a "sea-city" sited off the coast of Norfolk, around an artificial lagoon on the edge of a natural gas field. The wall enclosing the lagoon would be 180 ft. high, warding off all the cold winds, while the lagoon itself would be warmed to the temperature of the sea off the Scilly Isles. On the inside of the great wall of the lagoon would be sixteen levels of housing and industry, while other buildings, including houses, would be moored inside the lagoon. There would be escalators to carry people from one level to another; water buses and private transport would cross the lagoon and hovercraft and helibuses would keep the city in touch with the nearest land centre of Great Yarmouth, fifteen miles away.

Dreams? Those who live until the twenty-first century will know whether they have been merely that or not.

SELECT BIBLIOGRAPHY

ADDY, S. O.: *The Evolution of the English House,* Swan Sonnenschein (3rd edition), 1910

ARCHITECTURAL PRESS: *A Pocket Guide to the Buildings in Modern London.* 1951

BARLEY, M. W.: *The House and Home,* Vista Books, Longacre Press, 1963

BATSFORD, H. and FRY, C.: *The English Cottage,* Batsford, 1938

BAUER, CATHERINE: *Modern Housing,* Houghton Mifflin, N.Y., 1934

BRAUN, HUGH: *The Story of English Architecture,* Faber, 1950

BRETT-JAMES, N. G.: *The Growth of Stuart London,* Allen and Unwin, 1935

CHANCELLOR, E. BERESFORD: *The London of Dickens,* Grant Richards, 1924

CRANFIELD, S. W. and POTTER, H. J.: *Housing for the Working Classes in Urban Districts,* Batsford, 1900

DANNATT, TREVOR: *Modern Architecture in Britain,* Batsford, 1959

DESIGN AND INDUSTRIES ASSOCIATION: *Year Book 1929-30: The Face of the Land,* George Allen and Unwin

FORRESTER, HARRY: *The Timber-framed Houses of Essex,* Clarke (Chelmsford), 1959

FORRESTER, HARRY: *The smaller Queen Anne and Georgian House,* Clarke (Chelmsford), 1964

FOX, SIR C. and RAGLAN, LORD: *Monmouthshire Houses, a Study of Building Techniques (3 vols),* National Museum of Wales, 1951-4

GLOAG, JOHN: *The Englishman's Castle,* Eyre and Spottiswoode, 1944

HAMMOND, J. L. and BARBARA: *The Bleak Age,* Pelican, 1947

HAWKES C. and J.: *Prehistoric Britain,* Pelican, 1952

HENDERSON, ANDREW: *The Family House in England,* Phoenix, 1964

House and Garden Book of Cottages, 1963

INNOCENT, C. F.: *The Development of English Building Construction,* C.U.P., 1916

JONES, S. R.: *English Villages and Country Buildings,* Batsford, 1936

LLOYD, NATHANIEL: *A History of the English House,* Architectural Press, 1951

O'LEARY, J. G.: *The Book of Dagenham,* Borough of Dagenham, 1949

Observer, 18th February, 1968

PERCY, W. S.: *Strolling through Cottage England,* Collins, 1936

REDDAWAY, T. F.: *The Rebuilding of London after the Great Fire,* Cape, 1940

RICHARD, J. M.: *A Miniature History of the English House,* Architectural Press, 1938

RICHMOND (SURREY) BOROUGH OF: *Housing of the Working Classes,* 1899

SISSON, MARSHALL: *Country Cottages,* Methuen, 1949

TAYLOR, ALEC CLIFTON: *The Pattern of English Building,* Batsford, 1962

WALBANK, F. A.: *The English Scene,* Batsford (3rd edition), 1947

WALTON, JAMES: *Early timber Buildings of the Huddersfield District,* Tolson Memorial Museum, Huddersfield, 1955

INDEX

(Figures in italics indicate pages on which illustrations appear)